AFFIRMATIVE
ACTION

Positions:
EDUCATION, POLITICS, AND CULTURE
Edited by Kenneth J. Saltman, DePaul University,
and Ron Scapp, College of Mount St. Vincent

Affirmative Action:
RACIAL PREFERENCE IN BLACK AND WHITE
Tim J. Wise

The Edison Schools:
CORPORATE SCHOOLING AND THE ASSAULT
ON PUBLIC EDUCATION
Kenneth J. Saltman

AFFIRMATIVE
ACTION

RACIAL
PREFERENCE
IN BLACK
AND WHITE

TIM J. WISE

ROUTLEDGE
NEW YORK AND LONDON

Published in 2005 by
Routledge
Taylor & Francis Group
270 Madison Avenue
New York, NY 10016
www.routledge-ny.com

Published in Great Britain by
Routledge
Taylor & Francis Group
2 Park Square
Milton Park, Abingdon
Oxon OX14 4RN
www.routledge.co.uk

10 9 8 7 6 5 4 3 2 1

Library of Congress Cataloging-in-Publication Data
Wise, Tim J.
    Affirmative action : racial preference in black and white / Tim J. Wise.
        p. cm. -- (Positions : education, politics, and culture)
    Includes bibliographical references and index.
    ISBN 0-415-95048-1 (hardback : alk. paper) -- ISBN 0-415-95049-X
    (pbk. : alk. paper)
    1. Affirmative action programs in education--United States. 2. Discrimination
in higher education--United States. 3. Universities and colleges--United States--
Admission. I. Title. II. Series: Positions

    LC213.52.W57 2005
    379.2'6--dc22

                                                                    2004018897

CONTENTS

SERIES EDITORS' INTRODUCTION

Positions is a series interrogating the intersections of education, politics, and culture. Books in the series are short, polemical, and accessibly written, merging rigorous scholarship with politically engaged criticism. They focus on both pressing contemporary topics and historical issues that continue to define and inform the relationship between education and society.

"Positions" as a term refers to the obvious position that authors in the series take, but it might also refer to the "war of position" described by Italian cultural theorist Antonio Gramsci, who emphasized the centrality of political struggles over meanings, language, and ideas to the battle for civil society. We believe that these struggles over meanings, language, and ideas are crucial for the making of a more just social order in which political, cultural, and economic power is democratically controlled. We believe, as Paulo Freire emphasized, that there is no way not to take a position.

Tim Wise's book in the series, *Affirmative Action*, takes a position defending affirmative action policy against conservative calls for its dismantling. The book offers a clear and concise review of affirmative action policy, detailing the arguments for and against. The book illustrates the deep imbrications of racial and class oppression, thereby questioning approaches to affirmative action that view it exclusively as either an issue of culture or of economics. In keeping with the aims of the series, *Affirmative Action* not only offers a compelling argument replete with rich documentation to make the case for expanding affirmative action, but Tim Wise also reframes the very debate over affirmative action by suggesting that whites have been and continue to be the greatest recipients of affirmative action in the realms of schooling, employment, and housing. Wise calls for an end to the de facto affirmative action that white people accrue in part through an emphatic embrace of affirmative action for people of color. He suggests that policies that foster racial equality are a vitally necessary element of a democratic society and yet the only way to approach racial equality is to reverse the legacy of widely denied yet pervasively institutionalized white privilege.

KENNETH J. SALTMAN
ASSISTANT PROFESSOR, SOCIAL AND CULTURAL STUDIES IN EDUCATION
DEPAUL UNIVERSITY

RON SCAPP
ASSOCIATE PROFESSOR OF EDUCATION AND PHILOSOPHY
DIRECTOR OF THE MASTER'S PROGRAM IN URBAN AND
MULTICULTURAL EDUCATION
THE COLLEGE OF MOUNT ST. VINCENT

INTRODUCTION

In January 2003, President George W. Bush announced that his administration would be joining the legal battle against affirmative action at the University of Michigan. According to the president, Michigan's undergraduate College of Literature, Science, and the Arts, as well as its Law School, had devised unfair schemes of racial preference favoring blacks, Latino/as, and American Indians in admissions, relative to whites and Asians. Conjuring up the specter of "reverse discrimination," Bush insisted that admissions should be color-blind, and that Michigan, by way of its policies that considered, at least in part, an applicant's race when deciding whom to admit, had violated this color-blind ideal. In keeping with his belief that Michigan had violated both fairness and the Constitution, Bush instructed his Solicitor General to file arguments with the Supreme Court, on behalf of the white plaintiffs who had sued the University of Michigan and the law school, claiming to have been denied admission as a result of racial preferences for students of color.

In June of that year, the Supreme Court handed down a split decision, upholding affirmative action in the law school while striking down Michigan's undergraduate admission plan. The College of Literature, Science, and the Arts had been using a weighted point system, which automatically gave twenty points (out of an overall maximum of 150) to anyone who was a member of an underrepresented minority group, known as URMs. At Michigan, URMs are blacks, Latino/as, and American Indians, all of whom are statistically underrepresented, relative to their numbers in the potential applicant pool. Referred to as a de facto quota system by the plaintiffs and their attorneys, the point scheme was struck down as an unfair preference that placed an undue burden on white applicants, as well as Asian Pacific Islanders, who were not underrepresented at the University of Michigan. The law school program, although it considered race as one of many factors in admissions in an attempt to promote a diverse student body, had never operated with a point system. Because there was no explicit weighting on behalf of URMs in the law school, the Court upheld the constitutionality of the program, although narrowly, by a five to four vote.

Because the Court allowed schools to continue using race as a factor in admissions and yet struck down systems that use precise weighting for the purpose of expanding campus racial diversity, the controversy over affirmative action in higher education is sure to continue. It remains to be seen which affirmative action programs at which campuses will remain in place, which will be challenged in court, and which will be voluntarily abandoned for fear that they may be subject to legal challenge. In other words, given the split decision of the Supreme Court in the Michigan cases, the future of affirmative action in higher education remains up in the air.

So far the debate over affirmative action in education has divided into two camps, pretty well represented in the University of Michigan cases (*Gratz et al. v. Bollinger et al.* and *Grutter v. Bollinger et al.*). Those seeking to eliminate affirmative action label the practice "preferential treatment" or "racial preference," and claim that such efforts hold black, Latino/a, and American Indian applicants to lower standards, thereby unfairly punishing better-qualified whites (and, as we shall see, sometimes Asians), while harming those who receive the benefits, by casting them into academic waters they are ill-prepared to navigate.

On the other hand, defenders of affirmative action primarily argue that creating a diverse student body brings a range of benefits to students of all races, by exposing otherwise isolated persons to those from different backgrounds and experiences. Affirmative action supporters also argue that diversity improves the learning environment for all students and produces positive outcomes for graduates upon leaving college, such as greater involvement in civic affairs and a greater respect for others.

While the Supreme Court endorsed the "diversity defense" for affirmative action in the case of the University of Michigan Law School, it rejected the same argument in the undergraduate case because the point system the school was using was seen as too burdensome to students who were not members of URM groups, and an unconstitutional example of racial preference. But what the Court, and most other commentators have overlooked—and indeed what the defenders of affirmative action rarely point out either—is that the American educational system, from kindergarten through college, and beyond, perpetuates systemic racial preference and privilege, not for underrepresented minorities but, rather, for whites.

In this volume, I examine the larger structure of institutional white racial preference in American education and compare the magnitude of these preferences (affirmative action for whites, if you will) with the policies typically envisioned when the term *racial preference* is used. The purpose of such a comparison is to demonstrate that the educational system in the United States is both a reflection of and a contributor to the structure of institutionalized racism in this country, which works to the benefit of the dominant group and to the detriment of the persons supposedly receiving preference. This inquiry seeks to recast the way we conceive affirmative action.

Instead of seeing racial preference as something unique to the past thirty years, and uniquely offered to persons of color, I hope to demonstrate that preferential treatment for whites is not only woven throughout the history of the United States, but is also still very much in place. In other words, the question for those concerned about racial preferences is not, "Should we have racial preferences for people of color?" but, rather, "Should we *continue* to have racial preferences for whites?" Ultimately, I hope to make clear that unless the larger edifice of white racial preference is destroyed, it is far too premature to eliminate the relatively minor corrective efforts that we call affirmative action.

Although the system of racial preference that operates to the benefit of whites affects every realm of life in this country, not merely education—and I discuss some of the other arenas in which it plays out in the first chapter of this book—I chose to focus on schooling here for three reasons.

First, it is in the area of college admissions that affirmative action has been most recently in the news and on the minds of the public. Even before the decisions in *Gratz* and *Grutter*, there was the 1996 circuit court decision in *Hopwood v. Texas*, which tossed out affirmative action programs in three southern states. Although *Hopwood* has been trumped by the more recent Supreme Court rulings, the effect of several education-related affirmative action cases in the past few years, as well as publicity concerning the ban on affirmative action in the University of California system in 1995, has been to intensify the debate on affirmative action and to focus that debate principally within the arena of higher education.

Second, it is in the realm of college admissions where affirmative action often proves to be the most controversial. Because education is seen as a gateway opportunity, which is critical for accessing future opportunities in terms of jobs and careers, slots in colleges, law schools, medical schools, and graduate schools are highly coveted. These slots are far more limited than the slots for jobs, for example, and so the combination of scarcity and importance when it comes to obtaining an education can cause any effort to expand opportunities for one particular group to be viewed as a direct threat to others. Parents, highly protective of their children, and desiring them to succeed, are especially prone to opposing affirmative action in the educational arena, because slots at colleges and universities are seen, rightly or wrongly, as zero-sum: if blacks, for example, get more, whites get less. Therefore, because an education is so important to everyone's future, affirmative action becomes an easy target for conservative, and even some liberal, anger.

Finally, affirmative action, despite the recent Supreme Court rulings, is still probably more endangered in higher education than in the arenas of employment and contracting. Affirmative action for jobs and contracts is enshrined in federal law and spelled out quite clearly in terms of what is and is not required. Although, as shown below, these requirements are not particularly hard to meet, they are at least fairly detailed. However, educational institutions have always had far more leeway in devising their affirmative action programs. There really are no clear stipulations about what, if anything, is required of colleges and universities, which is probably the reason some schools have gotten in trouble for certain types of point systems, for example, and others have never come close to devising anything that dramatic. The danger of this imprecision is that it leaves colleges and universities in a state of limbo, which can then lead them to withdraw their affirmative action programs (even perfectly legal ones) voluntarily, out of a fear that their efforts may be met with a lawsuit. Because the contours of what is and is not allowed are constantly shifting, there is real concern among supporters of affirmative action that many schools may preemptively abolish their affirmative action efforts just to avoid trouble. As such, making the case for educational affirmative action is especially important as an antidote to the timidity that otherwise could sink many constructive equity efforts at colleges around the country.

This book is divided into three main chapters. In the first of these, I briefly examine how affirmative action programs, as commonly defined, operate (as opposed to how they are often presumed to operate), specifically in regard to employment and public contracting. Because the focus of the book is affirmative action in higher education and racial preference in the school system, I feel it necessary to also point out the way these efforts play out in the workforce, for three reasons: first, to dispel some common misconceptions about affirmative action in the employment realm, which often flow over into the attack on educational affirmative action; second, to set up the larger theme of this chapter, namely, that the history of this country has been the history of white racial preference—affirmative action for whites—in every realm of activity: law, jobs, housing. Furthermore, whites continue to reap the benefits of racial privilege in the job market today, as this chapter makes clear. And, finally, these preferences in the job market directly relate to preferences in the educational system, as discussed later in the volume, precisely because they allow white families to accumulate advantages in terms of housing and wealth that give their children a substantial head start when it comes time for school.

That whites typically ignore the embedded structures of racial preference that benefit them is not surprising, but is necessary to expose, nonetheless. By doing so and by first establishing a comprehensive framework for discussing the subject matter, we can move on to look at the way in which racial preference benefits whites in schools, and then respond to the critics of affirmative action.

In the book's second chapter, I examine the way institutional racism and white racial preference operate in the American educational system, from kindergarten to the highest levels of college and beyond. White racial dominance is maintained in schools by way of preexisting parental economic advantage; unequal resources available to schools serving mostly white students as opposed to those serving mostly students of color; so-called ability tracking, which tends to elevate whites and disadvantage blacks and Latino/as, irrespective of ability; and classroom and school cultures that favor white students at the expense of students of color.

Having sketched out a picture of racial preference far different from the one offered up by conservative critics of affirmative action programs, in the final chapter of the book I confront the litany of arguments made by those critics to attack the relatively paltry "preferences" in operation for the benefit of persons of color. In other words, whereas the previous chapter was the "offensive" case for affirmative action—that affirmative action is necessary to balance out the unjust advantages held by whites within the educational system in the United States—this chapter presents the "defensive" case by responding to the arguments most often made by those seeking to eliminate the programs.

First, I respond to the claim that affirmative action amounts to reverse discrimination against whites, thereby bumping whites from positions to which they are otherwise entitled. I pay special attention to the cases from the University of Michigan, both of which demonstrate the intellectually dishonest way that critics of affirmative action have sought to make their case.

Second, I tackle the argument that affirmative action in higher education lowers the standards for blacks, Latino/as, and American Indians, resulting in the admission of objectively less qualified students, and thereby harms these students by throwing them in over their heads at schools where they cannot compete.

Third, I respond to the claim that affirmative action stigmatizes its beneficiaries, making them always wonder whether their abilities are truly on par with those of others or whether they have only obtained their positions because of special preference. This argument, often made by black conservative critics of affirmative action, is presented as if to say that affirmative action should be abolished "for black folks' own good."

Fourth, I rebut the notion of the Asian "model minority." Critics of affirmative action have long been quick to point to the relative success of Asian Pacific Americans, when it comes to education and incomes, and argue that if Asians have "made it" in the United States, there is no reason blacks and other people of color cannot as well.

Finally, and somewhat related to the last point, I respond to the persistent claims by critics of affirmative action that the reason for black underachievement, underrepresentation in the best schools, and underemployment in the labor market is cultural deficiencies in the larger black community. This notion has become especially popular as a way to explain black underachievement in terms of academics, with conservatives blaming black students and families for insufficiently valuing education as a goal.

The book concludes with a discussion of how supporters of affirmative action might go about defending the concept, especially in a volatile political atmosphere, and what is problematic about the most common and currently popular way of doing so, which is to stress the benefits of diversity, be it in the workplace or on a college campus. While diversity in those and other settings no doubt has many positive features to recommend it, unless the defenders of affirmative action are willing to place affirmative action within the context of a larger social justice narrative—one that compares and contrasts these so-called preferences with the much larger edifice of white racial privilege and preference—it will be difficult to build or sustain a movement, either for the protection of affirmative action or for the eradication of racism.

The importance of putting forth a clear, social justice–oriented defense of affirmative action is all the more obvious given the opposition to such efforts: an opposition that is well-organized, well-financed, and dedicated to a highly ideological vision of American society, a vision in which the civil rights gains of the 1960s are reversed. Their own words make this clear, as with the Center for Individual Rights (or CIR), a conservative legal organization that has provided representation to white plaintiffs in "reverse discrimination cases." For several years, CIR boasted quite proudly on its Web site, "CIR advocates a limited application of civil rights laws that would preserve private citizens' right to deal with other private citizens without government scrutiny." In other words, CIR advocates the repeal of antidiscrimination laws that prevent companies or banks from discriminating against people of color, as well as laws that prevent housing discrimination by landlords or homeowners, or real estate agents, because all are "private" actors who, in the CIR estimation, should be able to do what they choose, without government scrutiny. Although this mission statement was removed from the CIR Web site in 2002, after appearing regularly since March 1999, there is little reason to believe that CIR actually altered its core beliefs in the intervening period. With an opposition so focused on rolling back the progress made by the civil rights movement, those of us dedicated to defending and extending those gains can hardly afford to be timid, to pull punches, or to limit our defense of affirmative action to mere pragmatic issues, such as the benefits of diversity.

Affirmative action is, as it has always been, about moving this nation toward racial equity and justice. That is what is at stake, and to ignore that basic truth is to imperil the victories of the past, and to diminish the opportunities for future victories.

1

AFFIRMATIVE ACTION PAST AND PRESENT

Affirmative action is perhaps one of the most misunderstood concepts in American politics today. Critics routinely characterize such efforts as "quotas," for example, despite the fact that affirmative action almost never involves quotas, and is far more modest than most people realize. Created in the 1960s and early 1970s as a way to ensure opportunity for people of color and white women who had been locked out of full participation in the job market and higher education, affirmative action programs have rarely required much in the way of concrete institutional change. If anything, although they have served as important reforms, affirmative action efforts have not gone nearly far enough, in light of how America's political, economic, and educational hierarchies remain so completely white dominated, as will be seen.

AFFIRMATIVE ACTION:
WHAT IT IS AND WHAT IT IS NOT

When it comes to educational institutions, nearly all college and university affirmative action programs were voluntarily adopted and have been limited in their approach to expanding access to historically underrepresented group members. The most common form of affirmative action in higher education is the deliberate and targeted recruitment of students of color, who otherwise might be overlooked by a particular school, despite their abilities and aptitudes. Additionally, schools often include race as one of many factors to consider when evaluating applicants, in that admissions officers will make note of race so that they might consider how the applicants' racial identity may have shaped their prior educational opportunities. For example, colleges might take a second look at an applicant of color, even if that applicant has lower test scores than a white applicant, if they can see that the applicant of color worked hard to achieve despite facing inferior educational resources and facilities. Although schools have occasionally set aside slots in an incoming class for students of color, or assigned weighted points to such students to increase the likelihood of obtaining a diverse student body, most efforts with this level of specificity have been eliminated, either by the courts, as with the Michigan undergraduate program, or voluntarily by schools worried that they might invite a lawsuit if they did not alter their existing policies.

In the realm of employment, affirmative action requirements, although more detailed than in higher education, are still far from onerous. As Fred Pincus explains in his recent book, *Reverse Discrimination: Dismantling the Myth*, affirmative action requirements apply only to certain companies, and even then, do not require very much of them. For example, nonconstruction companies with fifty or more employees and at least $50,000 in contracts with the government must have an affirmative action plan, but these plans do not have to be filed with the Equal Employment Opportunity Commission (EEOC) or any other agency. Furthermore, all the employers are required to do in the wake of developing such a plan is to make a "good faith effort" to hire members of whatever groups have been significantly underutilized relative to their availability in the qualified labor pool. In other words, affirmative action efforts are tied directly to how many people of color, for example, are available and qualified to do a certain job in a given location or industry. Because the job market for construction work is highly volatile, the requirements for construction companies are even more lax, and place very little emphasis on any kind of numerical goals or targets, even when there has been substantial underutilization of workers of color.

The only time that rigid numerical quotas are used is when a court has ordered them for a specified period, *after* a finding of discrimination against a particular firm, or after a given company has entered into a consent decree, in which they admit to having engaged in racial bias against persons of color, for example. At any given time, there are no more than a few dozen companies operating under such quota programs in the entire country.[1]

Not only are quota systems almost unheard of, but enforcement of the "good faith" efforts required by law is so weak that affirmative action is essentially voluntary in most cases. The Office of Federal Contract Compliance Programs (OFCCP), which is charged with monitoring affirmative action efforts, has only enough compliance officers to review about four thousand contractors annually, meaning that, at best, reviews could be done perhaps once every forty-six years for each company. Even worse, despite the regular discovery of firms that have violated antidiscrimination laws (both those pertaining to affirmative action and those merely requiring companies not to discriminate actively), fewer than fifty firms have been barred from participating in federal contracts because of failure to comply with affirmative action or antidiscrimination laws. Of those companies violating the law, sixty percent were ultimately reinstated as government contractors. In other words, enforcement is lax, the odds of getting caught discriminating are slim, and punishment, once a company is caught, is a joke, reducing the likelihood that affirmative action programs would operate, in practice, as a significant or even minor handicap to anyone.[2] This may well explain why discrimination continues to be so rampant, even among those businesses that are technically prohibited from engaging in it. As the OFCCP discovered in the mid-1990s, as many as three-quarters of all employers were in "substantial violation" of existing civil rights laws.[3]

Although the general public often perceives affirmative action requirements as tantamount to quotas, contractors covered by the requirements rarely see them that way. One 1995 survey of three hundred large federal contractors, for example, found that few viewed goals as quotas or unfair preference programs. Likewise, a 1994 customer satisfaction survey by the OFCCP found that only fourteen of 640 firms complained that they had felt pressured to use racial preference as a result of affirmative action requirements.[4] Unfortunately, contractors have often been found to have told rejected white male applicants that they were rejected because the contractor was forced to hire a woman or person of color, but no policy actually requires or encourages such an outcome.[5]

Affirmative action in contracting (such as for road construction or professional service contracts at the local, state, or federal level) generally refers to efforts that seek to steer a certain share of contract dollars to disadvantaged business enterprises (also known as DBEs). Companies owned by white men can also qualify as DBEs, so long as they can document some economic hardship or undercapitalization that has prevented them from full participation in private contracting markets. That said, it is certainly true that a disproportionate share of companies classified as DBEs are owned by either white women or men or women of color, in large part because DBE regulations have tended to presume that such businesses are disadvantaged—a reasonable assumption given the miniscule share of contracts and contract dollars going to such firms over the years, and still today. As will be seen, despite the presumption of disadvantage, which theoretically "preferences" contractors of color under DBE programs, only a very small share of public contracts are awarded to such companies, and there are no actual quotas for such contracting programs, but rather goals and timetables, pegged directly to the availability of minority- and women-owned businesses in a given locale.[6]

For the purposes of this volume, I define affirmative action as any race- or gender-conscious effort to identify, recruit, hire, admit, train, or promote qualified women or people of color for employment, educational, and contracting opportunities. Whereas standard antidiscrimination law takes a more passive approach, essentially saying that discrimination against a person on the basis of race, sex, or several other factors is illegal, affirmative action takes a more active stance. Affirmative action is essentially premised on the notion that without *deliberate* efforts to improve the representation of people of color and women of all colors, those individuals will continue to be overlooked, no matter what their talents and abilities.

UNDERSTANDING THE NEED: PREVENTING DISCRIMINATION, COUNTERING PREFERENCE

To many Americans, making deliberate efforts to include people of color in jobs, contracting, and educational institutions is unnecessary. After all, existing civil rights laws prohibit discrimination against persons of color, and that, they insist, should be enough to ensure equal opportunity. Yet as logical as such a position may seem, the inadequacy of such argumentation was explained by Martin Luther King, Jr., in his classic work, *Why We Can't Wait* (1963):

> Whenever this issue of compensatory or preferential treatment is raised, some of our friends recoil in horror. The Negro should be granted equality, they agree, but should ask for nothing more. On the surface, this appears reasonable, but is not realistic. For it is obvious that if a man enters the starting line of a race three hundred years after another man, the first would have to perform some incredible feat in order to catch up.[7]

In addition to the accumulated advantages of whites, and similarly accumulated disadvantages of blacks to which King was referring, there was also the reality that discrimination continued to take place, irrespective of the existence of new laws prohibiting it. Even with the Civil Rights Act of 1964, companies and contractors continued to block people of color from opportunities by way of subtle mechanisms, bogus "qualification" requirements, and reliance on "old boys networks" that were nearly all white thanks to decades of discrimination.[8] There were even companies that established "merit testing" for prospective employees only *after* the Civil Rights Act was passed, as a way to limit access for blacks artificially, as they could no longer blatantly discriminate against persons of color.[9] Unless these entities were required to make positive steps toward integrating their workforces, these people of color, no matter how qualified they might be, would continue to be locked out of the best opportunities. By the same token, whites would continue to be favored and preferenced in the job market.

Similarly, there were many subtle and often unintentional practices that also subverted and essentially served to circumvent civil rights legislation. For example, in the early 1960s it was quite common for employers to require referrals from existing employees for anyone seeking a job with their firm. Similarly, unions often restricted membership to family of existing union members. These and other practices had the effect of excluding people of color, whether deliberately or not, simply because of the history of previous exclusion that had restricted who would already be an employee or union member in the first place.[10]

Racial Discrimination and White Preference in the Job Market

Despite undisputed progress in opening up the job market to people of color over the past forty years, evidence of ongoing racial bias on the part of employers is clear at a number of levels, including who is interviewed for jobs after applying, who is hired, and how much money they earn, even when other factors like qualifications are the same between whites and job seekers of color.

Often, racial preference for whites in the workplace stems from subtle tendencies to favor those from one's own racial group when making a hiring decision. Studies have found that persons in a position to hire tend to spot merit most quickly in someone who reminds them of themselves,[11] and that members of dominant groups (especially in terms of race) have a particularly difficult time fairly evaluating the merit of minority group members, who are often viewed by whites in ways that fit common stereotypes.[12] As such, even if they are not overtly biased against people of color, because most hiring agents are white, they may tend to view other whites as more qualified, even when there is no objective evidence to justify such a belief. Studies have consistently found that people of color who are equally or more qualified than whites are still less likely to be hired because of racial prejudice on the part of employers or because those employers assume, despite evidence to the contrary, that the persons of color are less qualified.[13]

Even without overt bias operating to the advantage of whites and disadvantage of everyone else, white racial preference is also furthered in the job market by the workings of the so-called old boys network, which is often so important to landing the best jobs. More than eighty percent of executives find their jobs through networking, and almost nine in ten jobs in the overall labor market are filled by word of mouth and never advertised.[14] If these networks were race neutral, perhaps racial discrimination would be less of a problem. However, people of color are disproportionately excluded from the best word-of-mouth networks for jobs, due in large part to past inequity in hiring, housing and education, which has resulted in far fewer connections for people of color.[15]

There is also substantial evidence of ongoing direct discrimination against job applicants of color. As several studies have found, when discrimination "testers" (blacks and whites who are similarly dressed, are similarly qualified, and have similar demeanors) are sent out to apply for jobs and check for bias, whites receive interviews and job offers far more often than their black counterparts. One such study found that whites were twenty-two percent more likely to receive an interview and forty-five percent more likely to receive a job offer than equally qualified blacks.[16]

Another study in the Chicago suburbs, which paired slightly *more* qualified black women with slightly *less* qualified white women and had them apply for entry-level management positions with retailers, found similar results.[17] In tests that involved sending résumés only, but with no person-to-person interaction, researchers manipulated the names and home addresses of the applicants to signal that the applicant was either black or white. Overall, whites were twenty-one percent more likely to be granted an interview than their black co-testers, and employers were far more persistent in trying to reach white applicants than black applicants. Whites were almost twice as likely as blacks in the résumé-only tests to be blatantly preferred, despite having less objective experience and fewer credentials. In other words, in cases where one applicant received an interview while another did not, whites were on the winning end of that uneven equation almost twice as often as blacks, even when they were slightly *less qualified* than their counterparts of color.

In tests involving face-to-face contact with the potential employer, whites received job offers sixteen percent more often than blacks and, on average, were offered eight more hours per week than their black co-testers. Interestingly, although white and black in-person applicants were equally likely to be offered interviews, the kinds of questions asked of the various applicants nonetheless signified substantial if subtle racial preference for whites. For example, black applicants were far more likely to be quizzed by employers about why they wanted the job in question, and why they had left their previous job. Black applicants were four and one-half times more likely to be asked about their record with regard to absenteeism and punctuality, three times more likely to be asked how they had gotten along with previous supervisors, and two and one-half times more likely to be asked how they had gotten along in the past with co-workers. Such questions signify a long-established phenomenon, whereby white employers often view black workers suspiciously in terms of their interpersonal skills, work ethic, and motivation (so-called "soft-skills") even when their overall work experience is equal to or better than that of whites.[18]

Evidence suggests that discrimination is especially bad in suburbs, where black job applicants are hired approximately forty percent less often than whites, even when equally qualified, because of negative assumptions about blacks on the part of white employers.[19] Blacks looking for work in suburbs are hired at a rate that is roughly half their share of job applicants in the areas, whereas white applicants are hired at a rate that is twenty-two percent higher than their share of suburban job applicants.[20] Indeed, sociologist William Julius Wilson recently discovered that as many as three-quarters of white employers openly express negative views of black workers, irrespective of their firsthand experience with such employees.[21] Other studies suggest that one reason for such discrimination in white areas of town is that employers with a mostly white customer base are far less likely to feel comfortable hiring blacks and, as such, tend to do so far less often, regardless of qualifications.[22]

Going further than previous efforts, a large recent study by researchers at the University of Chicago and MIT found that when equally qualified job applicant résumés are sent to prospective employers, applicants with "white-sounding" names are fifty percent more likely to be called in for an interview than are applicants with "black-sounding" names. Interestingly, in the "names" study, while the odds of being called back for an interview rose as an applicant's credentials rose when the applicant was "white," for "black" applicants extra credentials did not seem to be of particular benefit, indicating that employers seem willing to pass over black job seekers even when they can tell that they are qualified and capable of performing the job in question.[23] Indeed, the researchers determined that merely having a white-sounding name was as valuable for job seekers (in terms of whether they received a callback) as having an additional *eight years* of work experience, and a black-sounding name.

Evidence even seems to indicate that whites with a criminal record often fare better in the job market than blacks *without* such a record. One study in Milwaukee, for example, had young black and white male job testers who were otherwise equally qualified apply for jobs in the metropolitan area. Some of the whites and some of the blacks claimed to have criminal records and to have served eighteen months in prison for possession of drugs with intent to distribute, while other whites and blacks presented themselves as having no prior criminal convictions.

Whites without records received callbacks for interviews thirty-four percent of the time, compared to only fourteen percent for blacks, and whites with criminal records received callbacks seventeen percent of the time, compared to only five percent for blacks with records. So whites without records were 2.4 times more likely than comparable blacks to receive an interview, and whites with criminal records were 3.4 times more likely to receive a callback than similar blacks. But even more amazingly, at seventeen percent, whites with prior drug convictions were more likely than blacks without records (at fourteen percent) to be called back for an interview, even when all other credentials were equal.[24]

Recent research by Alfred and Ruth Blumrosen, professors of law at Rutgers University, indicates that even using a very conservative methodology to screen out the kinds of racial and gender disparities that could occur by chance in the labor market, there are still about two million people of color and white women who will encounter discrimination in the workplace in any given year.[25]

None of this, of course, should be surprising. Despite improvements in the stated (or admitted to) levels of overt racism among whites, there are still large numbers of whites who adhere to negative views about blacks as a group, calling into question the degree to which whites holding such views could truly be expected to evaluate job applicants fairly. For example, although "only" thirteen percent of whites now admit to believing that blacks "lack an inborn ability to learn"[26] (which is an overtly racist concept), this represents roughly twenty-six million whites who feel that way. When we consider that there are likely others who agree with this statement but are savvy enough not to acknowledge such racism to pollsters (as doing so brands a person as less than enlightened in the modern era), it is quite possible that at least twenty percent of whites actually accept this racist notion. If so, that would mean that approximately forty million whites believe blacks to be inherently incapable of learning. Because there are only thirty-five million blacks in the United States, this would mean that for every African American in the country there was at least one white person who thought that blacks were inferior to whites—hardly a small concern.

Other surveys have indicated significant antiblack attitudes among whites, perhaps not as blatant as belief in inherent inferiority, but nonetheless troublesome. For example, according to a survey by the National Opinion Research Center, sixty-two percent of whites think blacks are generally lazier than other groups, fifty-six percent say they are more prone to violence, and fifty-three percent say they are generally less intelligent.[27]

Regardless of whether people believe they have a good reason to accept these views, the mere fact that most whites adhere to them means that it is nothing short of absurd to believe blacks would receive fair treatment in the labor market. After all, how can someone who believes blacks are lazy, less intelligent than whites, and prone to violence be expected to treat members of that stigmatized group equally with their white counterparts?

Beyond mere speculation, several experiments have borne out the notion that whites will often act on subtle, even subconscious biases, to the detriment of blacks applying for a job. In one particular study on hiring, researchers found that whites and blacks were treated equally when the information provided about them was either uniformly negative or uniformly positive. However, when applicants were presented to participants in the study as having a mix of positive and negative attributes, white applicants were significantly favored over their black counterparts. Such a result is consistent with the theory of "aversive racism," which is based on the idea that most people will act on racist beliefs only when they can reasonably explain away their actions as related to motives other than bias.[28]

In other words, when evaluating black applicants for a job, whites who are prejudiced will be more likely to treat them unfavorably when the blacks in question have some negative quality that can be used as the "real reason" for their exclusion. Yet white evaluators cut slack to whites with the same questionable attributes, indicating a tendency to magnify negatives for blacks while minimizing them for whites, in a way that systemically advantages the latter and damages opportunity for the former. Even though the treatment afforded to black and white applicants ends up clearly different, white evaluators can content themselves with the idea that their actions were not racist because there were ostensibly nonracial reasons for their decision making, however flimsy those alternative rationales might actually have been.

Income and Employment Disparities as Evidence of White Preference

Racial discrimination and white racial preference can also be inferred from data on relative racial rates of employment and earnings. Although not all gaps in economic status are the result of racism, persistent disparities even among those with equal qualifications call into question the degree to which hiring and pay scales are merely the result of relative merit. When equally or more-qualified blacks are less likely to have jobs than whites, or when they earn less, especially much less, the likelihood that racial discrimination is operating is high.

Racial earnings gaps continue to persist at all levels of education and across all types of professions. According to the Integrated Public Use Microdata Series of the Census Bureau, whites with high school diplomas, college degrees, or master's degrees all earn approximately twenty percent more than their black counterparts. Even more striking, whites with professional degrees (such as degrees in medicine or law) earn, on average, thirty-one percent more than similar blacks and fifty-two percent more than similar Latino/as.[29] Even when other factors that could affect wages are the same between blacks and whites, like experience, seniority, education, and geographic location (factors that are hardly independent of racism), the wage gap between whites and blacks remains between ten and twenty percent.[30]

Looking at whites and blacks of similar age, doing the same work, earnings gaps remain significant. In fact, even if we look only at the youngest cohorts of whites and blacks, this remains true: an important fact, because those persons between the ages of twenty-five and thirty-four would have had more equal opportunities than their parents' and grandparents' generations. Among those twenty-five to thirty-four years old, white lawyers earn, on average, twenty-three percent more than comparable blacks; white doctors and surgeons earn, on average, one-third more than comparable blacks; white computer programmers earn, on average, twenty-two percent more than comparable blacks; white carpenters earn, on average, twenty-four percent more than comparable blacks; white accountants earn, on average, thirty-one percent more than comparable blacks; and even white janitors earn sixteen percent more, on average, than comparable blacks.[31] Although these gaps do not necessarily reflect overt and deliberate discrimination by given employers—they could, for example, illustrate the largely segmented nature of the labor market, whereby whites have greater access to more lucrative clients and companies—the effect is the same. Irrespective of experience and education, whites continue to receive advantages in the labor market over equally qualified blacks.

Census data on employment and earnings suggest that whites continue to be racially preferred in the labor market, even when compared to persons of color who are their equals in terms of educational background. Black college graduates, for example, are only two-thirds as likely as white graduates to be employed in professional or managerial jobs, while Latino/a college graduates are only forty-four percent as likely to be professionally or managerially employed. Likewise, the median earnings of black college graduates who work year round, full-time are only eighty-seven percent of white median earnings at the same level of education, and median earnings for Latino/a college graduates are only eighty-four percent of the white median.[32]

Conservatives, of course, have ready excuses for these persistent wage gaps, even in the wake of equivalent educations between whites and blacks. For example, it is sometimes suggested that blacks earn less, despite having the same terminal degree as whites, because blacks major in less lucrative subjects. But in truth, blacks are slightly more likely than whites to get a degree in the relatively lucrative areas of business, computer science, or mathematics, only slightly less likely to get a degree in the natural sciences,[33] and less likely to major in the relatively less lucrative social science fields associated with liberal arts degrees.[34] Although a slightly larger share of black graduates major in education—an admittedly lower-paying profession than many others—the white/black differences here are not dramatic: about twenty-one percent of black college graduates majored in education, compared to seventeen percent of whites.[35] The only substantial difference between whites and blacks in terms of the coursework taken in college is found in the percentages of each receiving a degree in engineering, which is, of course, an extremely lucrative discipline and future career choice. Here, whites are 2.6 times more likely than blacks to receive an engineering degree. But even then, as only seven percent of whites received degrees in this area, it is hardly realistic to expect that this could make a considerable difference to overall racial wage gaps.[36]

Some on the right then claim that earnings gaps merely reflect different cognitive abilities, as reflected in grades and test scores; in other words, even if blacks and whites have the same terminal degree, and more or less the same majors, if blacks do worse in those classes, or on standardized tests, they should be expected to earn less. Although it is true that black grade-point averages in college tend to lag behind whites (for reasons to be discussed in Chapter Three), thirty-five different studies have confirmed that, at most, grades and scores on standardized tests can perhaps explain three percent of income variances between any two workers—hardly sufficient to explain the gaps that separate whites and blacks in the labor market.[37] Even after controlling for racial differences in so-called cognitive ability, family background, and other factors, white males receive up to seventeen percent higher wages than otherwise identical black male heads of households.[38] Likewise, other wage comparisons of blacks and whites who graduated from selective colleges and universities have found that even after controlling for differences in grades, college majors, and socioeconomic status, whites consistently earn more and blacks significantly less.[39]

If anything, then, affirmative action's biggest problem is that it has not done *enough* to root out white racial preference in the job market.

Contracting, Business Opportunity, and White Preference

As with employment, affirmative action in contracting has hardly altered, in any fundamental way, the dominant position of white male-owned businesses when it comes to procuring government contracts. Although people of color own fifteen percent of all businesses in the United States, they receive only 6.2 percent of federal contract dollars. White women, also covered by affirmative action programs in contracting, own thirty-eight percent of all businesses, yet receive only 2.3 percent of federal contracts. In other words, white male-owned companies receive roughly 91.5 percent of all federal contract dollars, despite representing only forty-seven percent of all businesses in the nation.[40]

Although affirmative action in contracting was opening municipal contracting opportunities to people of color prior to restrictions imposed by the Supreme Court in the late 1980s, since that time the picture has become dismal. Consider Richmond, Virginia: When the Supreme Court threw out the city's affirmative action plan in 1989, the share of contracts going to black-owned companies fell from thirty-eight percent of the total to only 2.2 percent.[41] Although these numbers have rebounded a bit, to around eleven percent, the decision by the Court had a substantial impact on black business opportunity, as in Philadelphia, where the share of city contracts going to minorities fell from twenty-five to 3.5 percent, or in Tampa, where the use of minority firms for municipal contracts essentially ended altogether after the decision.[42] In none of these cases was there evidence that the minority contractors had done inferior or noncompetitive work. It appeared simply as if white contractors no longer would work with people of color unless required to do so, preferring to work with those in preexisting old boys networks, much to the detriment of true equal opportunity.

Even before the point of procuring federal contracts, however, there is the more basic issue of white racial preference in obtaining business loans from banks in the first place, so as to operate at all. One study, conducted by researchers at the University of Colorado at Boulder, found that blacks seeking business loans are two to three times more likely to be rejected than whites, and at the highest levels of assets and collateral, blacks are twelve times more likely to be turned down than whites.[43]

Of course, that people of color find themselves at a disadvantage and whites at an advantage within the larger opportunity structure in the United States should come as no surprise. After all, not only does discrimination in the present take place, as we've seen, but we are still living with the legacy of institutionalized racial oppression, a subject to which we now turn. Without an understanding of this legacy and the way in which it has always provided racial preference to whites and allowed white racial privilege to become ingrained over time, any discussion of affirmative action will, by definition, be incomplete.

RACIAL PREFERENCE IN HISTORY: A LOOK AT AFFIRMATIVE ACTION FOR WHITES

What few whites seem to comprehend is just how entrenched racial preference has been in the history of the United States and, more to the point, how *white* the face of that preference has looked. Understanding the history of racial preference for whites is important to the affirmative action debate for at least two reasons. First, it places existing efforts for people of color within their proper historical context, thereby obviating the notion that they amount to some unique break with color-blind meritocracy. Second, it allows a more honest discussion of the legitimacy of such programs, since had it not been for the history of white racial preference and privilege, affirmative action for people of color would never have come into being in the first place. As obvious as it might seem that America's history has been one of overt racial preference for whites, many conservatives continue to act as if it has only been with the intro-duction of affirmative action for people of color that race has played a role in dispensing opportunity. As Terry Eastland argues in his book, Ending Affirmative Action, "Affirmative action broke with the color-blind tradition," which in his mind (although surely not in history) "stretches back to the American foundation."[44]

Whiteness Preferenced in American Law and Custom

That whites like Eastland fail to see the way in which white racial preference operates, and has always operated, in this country is no surprise. After all, Justice Joseph Bradley, writing for the

Supreme Court in an 1883 decision invalidating several civil rights provisions that had been passed in the wake of the Civil War, noted, without any sense of irony, that the post-emancipation civil rights laws were unfair preferential treatment. He went so far as to argue that blacks should, just two decades after emancipation, cease being the "special favorite of the laws" and take their place among "mere citizens." That whites were not "mere citizens" but, rather, favored citizens, with huge advantages that had been cemented in place for generations, completely escaped the Court.[45]

The Court's reasoning was similar to that of President Andrew Johnson, who explained his decision to veto the 1866 Civil Rights Act on the grounds that its provisions for creating a modicum of opportunity for the former slaves were "infinitely beyond any that the Central Government have ever provided for the white race." That the white race had never needed specific provisions delineating its opportunities and safeguarding them, since it was the dominant group in charge of every institution, was, to Johnson, a matter of no relevance whatsoever.[46]

Today, we can regularly hear similar arguments being made by critics of affirmative action, who suggest that blacks should "work their way up like the Irish, Italians and Jews, without any special favors,"[47] ignoring, of course, that the ability of those groups' members to become white, and to assimilate into the larger umbrella of the "white race," was itself a "special favor."[48]

Preferential treatment for whites has, of course, been the hallmark of American law and society for hundreds of years. In fact, the very introduction of the term "white" to describe Europeans took place in the context of extending opportunities and legal immunities to persons so designated, opportunities and immunities that were equally denied to blacks. By the 1690s, and first few years of the eighteenth century, as colonies like Virginia began to enshrine permanent slavery for blacks and to phase out European indentured servitude (and to place lower-income whites on slave patrols to control blacks), the privileging of those called white was well on its way to becoming fully entrenched in the policies of what would later become the United States.[49]

Preferential treatment for whites continued with Article IV of the Constitution, which provided for the return of fugitive slaves to their masters, thereby elevating the property rights of whites over and above the human right of persons to be free from bondage. It would be reinforced yet again, after the Constitution's ratification, when the first Congress passed the Naturalization Act of 1790, which specified that "free white persons" (and only free white persons) were eligible to become full citizens of the nation. Surely, this was an act of affirmative action and racial preference.[50]

White racial preference was also enshrined in the Homestead Act of 1862, which allowed whites, but typically not people of color, to lay claim to up to 160 acres, for only a $10 downpayment.[51] In later years, "affirmative action" for whites would continue, in the form of immigration preferences that allowed Europeans to come to the United States in far greater numbers than people of color; labor laws that preserved the right of white unions to exclude people of color from their ranks; Social Security provisions that for many years after their inception excluded agricultural laborers and domestic workers from qualifying for retirement benefits (thereby excluding most blacks and boosting the retirement picture for whites relative to people of color); and of course, segregation laws that would remain in effect, legally, until the 1960s.[52]

Together, these laws and policies elevated whites—not some, it should be stressed, but all whites—above the status of persons of color. As harsh as conditions were for many European immigrants, and as unjust as the discrimination to which they were subjected most certainly was, it is nonetheless the case that their very ability to enter the United States when they did, and to obtain a number of jobs that were off-limits to blacks and other persons of color, were the result of white racial preference. Even the most despised of European "ethnics" could become white over time, a process of racial matriculation that was essentially impossible for anyone of color.

Federal Housing Policy as White Racial Preference

One of the clearest examples of racial preference for whites occurred in the recent past and involved the way in which housing became available to whites, but typically not to people of color, during the middle of the twentieth century. In the 1930s, the government began offering low-interest, taxpayer-guaranteed, and underwritten loans through the Federal Housing Administration (FHA) loan program. The FHA program, and a similar program for veterans in later years, was premised on the notion that building a middle class of productive, upwardly mobile homeowners would require a jumpstart from the government. Banks were too concerned with possible defaults to write mortgages for moderate-income families prior to that time, but with government guarantees in place, their willingness blossomed. Millions of families from the 1930s to the 1960s took part in the new housing programs, and the American middle class was born. Over a thirty-year period in the middle of the century, more than $100 billion in home equity was loaned through these housing initiatives, boosting the overall rate of homeownership from a mere forty-four percent in 1934 to nearly two-thirds by 1969.[53]

But it was almost exclusively a white middle class created by these policies. FHA lending guidelines, written by the Home Ownership Lending Corporation (HOLC), made it very clear that these preferential loans were off-limits to persons who lived in "declining" neighborhoods (and every black neighborhood was rated as declining), and that loans were also to be denied to anyone whose receipt of the loan would result in a reduction in a neighborhood's racial homogeneity. Specifically, the FHA underwriting manual explained to lenders, "If a neighborhood is to retain stability, it is necessary that properties shall continue to be occupied by the same social and racial classes."[54] In other words, there would be few if any loans for blacks seeking to move to mostly white areas either.

So blacks were restricted to the urban core at the very time that the "American dream" was being subsidized for white families via the FHA and VA loan programs. Even black veterans were regularly turned down for loans in white suburbs. As a result of the blatant discrimination in housing during this period, twenty-seven million of the twenty-eight million Americans who moved into suburban areas from 1950 until 1966 were white. This in turn proved a huge economic windfall for whites, as roughly eighty percent of all new jobs being created in emerging sectors of the economy were created in the suburbs, where for the most part only they could live.[55]

From the end of World War II to the early 1960s, the FHA and VA loan programs for housing, both of which operated in a racially restrictive manner, funded more than a third of all mortgages written, and assisted in the building of almost half of all suburban housing built in the period, housing that was basically off-limits to anyone who was not white.[56] By 1960, forty percent of all white mortgages were being written through the preferential FHA and VA loan programs.[57] And of course, even those mortgages obtained by whites without FHA or VA assistance were obtained preferentially, as people of color were largely locked out of the conventional loan market as a result of overt discrimination and many of the same assumptions about "neighborhood stability" that had animated the original HOLC guidelines in use by the government.

Importantly, as white housing was being subsidized, housing for people of color was being destroyed. In the 1950s, local governments began the process of "urban renewal," which typically meant the elimination of low- and moderate-income family housing, to be replaced by office buildings, shopping centers, and parking lots. While hundreds of thousands of homes (amounting to one-fifth of all housing occupied at the time by people of color)[58] were destroyed as part of this process, less than ten percent of those displaced—three-fourths of whom were black—had new single-residence housing to go to afterward, as cities rarely built new units to replace the old ones. Instead, displaced families often had to rely on crowded apartments, living with relatives, or living in run-down public housing projects.[59]

ONGOING HOUSING BIAS AND THE ACCUMULATION OF WHITE WEALTH

Even with the Fair Housing Act of 1968, ostensibly guaranteeing an end to racial discrimination in housing, all available evidence indicates that blacks and other people of color are still not truly free to live where they choose. According to federal estimates, as many as two million cases of housing discrimination take place every year against persons of color.[60] These acts of discrimination range from outright bias in mortgage lending, to refusing to show apartments to people of color, to steering blacks to mostly black neighborhoods, to showing fewer units to blacks seeking to rent or fewer homes to those seeking to buy. In large part because of past and present racial bias in housing markets, even blacks in northern cities with annual incomes of $50,000 are just as likely to live in segregated neighborhoods as blacks earning only $2,500 annually.[61]

The head start afforded to millions of whites because of these housing preferences, among other programs, has paid dividends in the current generation that are far from insubstantial. Even though young two-earner black couples have substantially reduced the income gap between themselves and young two-earner white couples of similar educational background, their life situations remain quite different, thanks to the effects of past racism. Because the parents and grandparents of young whites were able to accumulate assets and professional security at a time when the parents and grandparents of blacks were restricted in their ability to do the same, today's young black couples, although earning roughly the same as whites on the job, continue to have a net worth that is less than one-fifth the worth of young white couples.[62]

Because of the cumulative effects of longstanding racial discrimination and direct barriers to black capital formation, white households are far more likely to inherit or otherwise benefit from family wealth than black households. Several studies have examined the racial gaps in inherited assets and concluded that whites are between 2.2 and 3 times more likely than blacks to receive an inheritance or other form of intergenerational wealth transfer, and that the average value of inheritances received by whites is as much as 3.6 times higher than the value of inheritances received by blacks.[63] Today, the typical white family has wealth and net worth that is nearly eleven times that of the typical black family, and eight times higher than the typical Latino/a family.[64] Because accumulated family wealth is one of the principal methods by which parents pay for their children's college education, this economic head start then directly privileges whites as a group when it comes time for higher education as well.[65]

WHITE DENIAL, AMBIVALENCE, AND "REVERSE DISCRIMINATION"

Despite evidence such as that above, eighty percent of whites deny that racial discrimination against people of color is a significant problem, and by extension that they receive any kind of advantages as a result.[66] According to one poll, taken by The Washington Post, six in ten whites say blacks are as well off or better off than whites when it comes to educational opportunity, and eighty percent say blacks are as well off or better off than whites when it comes to jobs and income.[67]

Not only do whites deny the severity of the problem of racism, they also exhibit a marked indifference and ambivalence to issues of racial equity. One-third of whites, for example (which amounts to nearly seventy million whites in all), say it's "not that big a problem" if some people have more of a chance in life than others. Although only thirteen percent of whites said they had "no interest" in issues of equal opportunity, when asked in 1964, by the mid-1980s, the percentage of whites saying they had no interest in the issue had risen to one-third. Even more disturbing, while almost all whites say they agree with the idea that whites and people of color should have an equal opportunity to obtain any job, fewer than half of whites say the government should do anything to ensure fair treatment for all in the employment arena. In other words, most whites today reject the notion that the government should play any role in preventing discrimination, let alone enforcing affirmative action laws.[68]

Against this backdrop of ambivalence and denial is the ubiquitous drumbeat of so-called reverse discrimination. In fact, when asked which is the bigger problem, discrimination against people of color or "reverse discrimination" against whites, whites are twice as likely to say the latter.[69] Interestingly, however, despite their belief in the regularity of so-called reverse discrimination, few whites believe they have personally been the victims of such a phenomenon, with no more than thirteen percent, and often as few as two percent saying that they have ever lost a job, for any reason, to a less-qualified person of color or white woman. Consistent with this data, only a very small percentage, about four percent, of all discrimination claims filed with the EEOC are filed by whites alleging racial discrimination, and three-quarters of these have nothing to do with complaints about the effects of affirmative action programs, but, rather, concern claims of unfair treatment on the job, or unfair dismissals, or other forms of harassment.

From 1995 to 2000, the EEOC resolved more than 183,000 cases involving alleged racial discrimination, of which nearly 167,000 were brought by people of color, and slightly fewer than 17,000 were claims brought by whites. In other words, there were approximately ten times more discrimination claims brought by people of color than by whites, even though whites make up a much larger share of the labor force.[70] Furthermore, discrimination claims brought by whites are typically less credible than those brought by persons of color, with the latter seventy-two percent more likely to succeed in court.[71]

Taken together, what both history and contemporary evidence indicate is that racial preference is a very real thing, but that its primary beneficiaries, at least in jobs, contracting, and housing, are white. Not only have laws and customs provided immense privileges and head starts to whites in the past, but current discrimination also continues to hold back persons of color, relative to their abilities, desires, and talents. The advantages enjoyed historically and still today, in terms of jobs, income, housing, and business opportunities, have not only amounted to significant benefits in their own right, but have also borne substantial benefits to the children of those so preferenced, in terms of education: the kind of schools such children would attend, the resources available for their educations, and their likelihood of attending college. It is in this sense that racial preference for whites in the larger economy is directly related to white racial preference in education, resulting in a cyclical pattern, whereby prior economic advantage produces educational advantage, which in turn replicates economic dominance, in an intergenerational process. It is to the subject of white racial preference in education that we now turn.

Just as with critiques of affirmative action in jobs and contracting, there is much misunderstanding of these efforts in the realm of education. These misunderstandings and outright distortions are addressed in Chapter Three, but for now we should first examine the rarely discussed but disturbing reality that the primary racial preference in the arena of education is hardly that provided to people of color by way of affirmative action: rather, it is the systemic and institutionalized racial preference afforded to whites at all levels of schooling.

2

WHITE RACIAL PREFERENCE
IN EDUCATION

To say that the American educational system is one in which racial preference was ingrained for whites, historically, would be an understatement of monumental proportions. In truth, there was essentially no broad-based public education system for blacks *at all* until the 1920s, and even then, it was separate and unequal in the extreme.[1] Southern states for generations made it illegal to teach black slaves how to read English, and even outside of the South there was simply no formal educational opportunity to speak of for the vast majority of African Americans until the twentieth century.

Indeed, contrary to common perceptions that education is meant to be the "great equalizer," allowing individuals to rise to the level of their abilities, schooling in the United States has always been constructed to maintain existing hierarchies and divisions, with regard to not only race but also class status. It was Thomas Jefferson who advocated three years of compulsory schooling for all, to "rake a few geniuses from the rubbish"[2] (the implicit assumption was that the bulk of the citizenry would indeed remain at the bottom of the rubbish pile), and it was Woodrow Wilson who, as president of Princeton University, once explained, "We want one class of persons to have a liberal education and we want another class of persons, a very much larger class of necessity in every society, to forego the privilege of a liberal education and fit themselves to perform specific difficult manual tasks."[3] In other words, education was not for everyone.

Although we may think that America's educational system, however unequal it once was, now seeks to promote equality, nothing could be further from the truth. First, it should be noted that despite evidence to the contrary, white Americans have long believed the nation's educational system to be a fair and equitable one, even at times when most everyone today would see the absurdity in such a claim. Virtually all would agree today that the nation's schools were profoundly unequal in the early 1960s—this was just a few years after the Supreme Court had struck down segregation in the historic Brown v. Board of Education decision, and long before most school systems had actually begun to remove the vestiges of separate and unequal education—yet, at the time, whites by and large felt there was nothing wrong. As hard as it may be to believe in retrospect, in 1962, more than nine in ten whites told pollsters that blacks had just as good a chance for a quality education as they did.[4] In other words, our faith in equal opportunity has long outstripped the reality.

Today, although our faith in educational equity is even stronger than it once was, there are still quite deliberate mechanisms by which inequality is maintained. As education reformer, Alfie

Kohn, explains, today's emphasis on standardized testing is intended to replicate substantial disparities between students. If too many students do well, teachers are accused of grade inflation and tests are retooled to be more difficult. Low scores and large gaps between test takers are what mark tests as legitimate, which means that the purpose of "tougher standards," is really to produce and maintain inequality. In other words, increased failure is proof of *success!*[5]

Since most standardized tests are norm-referenced, meaning they are scored in relation to the median test score, not an objective, or universal standard related to the number of right and wrong answers, the outcome of such tests will be guaranteed inequality. Such tests are designed so that ten percent of all students, for example, will be in the top ten percent of scorers, and half of all students who take the test will fall below the median. In other words, norm-referenced tests presume at the outset that skills and abilities fall along a bell-shaped curve, with a few students at the top, a few at the bottom, and most in the middle, even though there is no objective basis for this presumption, especially for each and every skill test administered. The problem with such an assumption is that because students must be fit into slots relative to the "norm," very small gaps in actual knowledge could produce large gaps in test scores, simply to fit within the preset curve. Inequality, then, is manufactured quite deliberately, regardless of what it may actually tell us about student abilities. And, it should be noted, because white, middle-class students typically set the "norm," students of color will almost always operate at a disadvantage in a school system that emphasizes these kinds of cognitive testing instruments.

But the problem is not merely testing. An examination of the educational system in the United States reveals multiple levels at which white racial preference is replicated. These include the highly unequal starting points for white students versus those of color, due to parental advantage and the concentration of poverty in schools attended by so many students of color; the misuse of so-called ability tracking, which blatantly favors white students and disadvantages students of color; and classroom cultures and teaching styles that result in the preferencing of whites to the detriment of students of color. As a result of these and other factors, when it comes time for students to apply for college, the rarely acknowledged but nonetheless disturbing truth is that it is whites and not students of color who receive the largest "preferences" and advantages.

Although there are observable academic performance differences between white and black students as early as kindergarten, the clear consensus of existing research suggests that these differences are smaller in the earliest years of schooling, and grow substantially over time.[6] Indeed, although the percentages of blacks, whites, and Latinos who score at least one year below grade level are roughly equivalent between the ages of 6 and 8, by the time students reach their teenage years, the percentages of students of color who lag at least a year behind grade level well exceed the percentages for whites.[7] Despite little change in home environment from the time they are young until the time they are teens, African American and Latino/a students fall farther and farther behind relative to their white peers as their schooling goes along, suggesting strongly that something is happening in the schools that produces this result.

PREEXISTING FAMILY ADVANTAGE AS RACIAL PREFERENCE

There is little doubt but that black students face substantially greater hardships and disadvantages than their white counterparts; indeed, the average black teenager lives in a neighborhood with a poverty rate of seventeen percent, more than double the rate for the average white teen's community. Likewise, the average black high school student attends a school with twice as many low-income students as the typical white student.[8]

Seventy percent of all students of color attend schools with people of color majorities, half of all black students are in schools that are at least seventy-five percent people of color,[9] and one-third attend schools that are at least ninety percent nonwhite.[10] Despite reductions in school segregation in the 1970s, the trend since that time has been consistently backward, such that blacks are as segregated today, away and apart from white students, as they were in 1971, before the beginning of widespread busing.[11] This is especially true for urban blacks in large cities, more than ninety-two percent of whom attend mostly, if not all black schools.[12] Likewise, half of white students attend schools that are ninety percent or more white, and seven in ten whites attend schools with fewer than one-quarter students of color.[13]

Most problematic about this educational resegregation from the perspective of white racial privilege and black and brown disadvantage is that while schools with large concentrations of black and brown students tend to be places with high levels of concentrated poverty, schools with student bodies that are eighty percent or more white are rarely high-poverty schools. In fact, they are only about seven percent as likely to attend concentrated poverty schools as their black and brown counterparts, signifying a huge advantage for whites in such locations.[14]

Even blacks with incomes higher than whites are less likely to attend high-quality schools[15] and more likely to live in low-income neighborhoods,[16] and their families, on average, have far less net worth and wealth reserves than whites with high incomes.[17] One study of black youth in Philadelphia found that black children from affluent families typically attend school with three times more low-achieving poor students than affluent white children, due to long-standing housing segregation and unequal access to quality schools.[18]

The effect of attending concentrated poverty schools is substantial, even for those students who are not poor themselves, and tends to result in lower scores on standardized tests, irrespective of family economic position.[19] The concentration of poverty in black and brown schools magnifies any number of social problems, including inadequate nutrition and health care, family problems including unemployment or low-wage employment, and the emotional costs associated with growing up in marginalized and isolated places without the kinds of connections to opportunity enjoyed by students in more stable communities. This means that black students with more family income will still face obstacles as a result of racial isolation and de facto segregation. So even relative to blacks of comparable economic status, white students and their families experience privilege and racial preference.

Hypersegregation also affects Latino/a students. Three of four Latino/a students attend schools with people of color majorities, and more than a third are highly segregated, in places where students of color make up ninety percent or more of the student bodies. These schools are eleven times more likely than ninety-percent white schools to be schools with high concentrations of poverty.[20]

The persistent resegregation of American schools has tended to magnify and replicate white racial privilege for the group as a whole, given the class advantages that whites so often enjoy relative to students of color. Exposure to low-quality educational resources, as so often happens in hypersegregated high-poverty schools, can have a profound effect on a child's cognitive development. Indeed, children can suffer a loss of up to six points on an IQ test, relative to what they would have scored, for every year they are subjected to substandard resources, instruction, and educational facilities.[21] Then, having scored lower on such tests, they will be labeled as less capable students, tracked into remedial-level courses, exposed to less challenging work, and thus ultimately fulfill the low expectations placed on them as a result of their initial disempowerment.

Not only do preexisting economic cleavages tend to favor whites at the expense of youth of color, but there are also subtle ways in which whites are able to access preference and privilege within the schools because of their backgrounds. For example, white students reap the benefits of parents who are more likely to know how to access outside assistance, and be able to pay for that assistance, if and when their child is struggling. They are more likely to feel confident demanding help for their child and, because of greater average levels of education and professional status, to be in a position to follow through and ensure that all that can be done for their child is done, on those occasions when they may be having trouble in school.[22] White parents also often have an inside track in placing their kids into the better "alternative" schools within their urban systems, due to a familiarity with the forms involved and the process for accessing these kinds of special opportunities.[23] These advantages are especially pertinent in relation to parents whose primary language is not English, as with Latino/a immigrants and their children.

Similarly, white students reap the benefits of having parents who are more likely to be able to add resources to their schools, through PTAs or other fund-raising efforts. They are also more likely than their black or brown counterparts to have parents who can volunteer at their schools, and thus provide more human resources to the institution, because of a greater likelihood of having a parent who does not have to work in the paid labor force. In other words, the preexisting class advantages of whites as a group translate into substantial advantages for their white children in school, advantages that cannot be ignored as we examine the issue of unfair racial preference.

Other benefits obtain to white students as a result of their parent's class status as well. To the extent that parental socioeconomic status is a key factor in literacy and academic achievement worldwide,[24] there is little doubt but that whites will have an edge going into school and throughout the educational process, relative to students of color, whose families are substantially more likely than white families to be poor. Studies have found that reading achievement gaps between whites and blacks can be entirely explained by the socioeconomic disparities existing in respective white and black households, specifically, because during summer vacations whites—disproportionately from more affluent families—are able to receive more reinforcement and academic stimulation than black and brown children of school age.[25]

FUNDING AND RESOURCE DISPARITIES AS WHITE RACIAL PREFERENCE

Among the most obvious examples of white racial preference in the educational arena is the persistent resource disparity between schools that serve mostly whites and those that serve students of color. Although conservatives often point to raw per-pupil spending data that indicate that roughly equivalent amounts of money are spent per pupil in poor and mostly person of color districts as in whiter and wealthier districts,[26] such comparisons are misleading.

First, costs for everything from supplies, to school maintenance, to transportation, to employee compensation are higher in larger urban districts, which educate a disproportionate share of low-income and minority students. So a dollar in a suburban or rural area stretches farther than in an urban center, meaning that, if anything, urban schools require more money to achieve the same result. Similarly, large urban districts with significant numbers of low-income students tend to have a far larger share of students with disabilities, the education of which also costs more than education for students without special needs. And, finally, it has long been an accepted principle among education experts that educating low-income students costs more than educating affluent students, because the former face so many problems and obstacles not faced by the latter and have fewer resources outside of school that they can call upon to supplement their formal schooling.

As a general rule, it has long been understood that educating poor students requires spending at least twenty percent more than educating nonpoor students. But even that assumption is conservative. Indeed, recent federal law actually provides funding incentives for local school districts, which assume those districts should spend forty percent more for the education of poor students to be truly providing equal educational opportunity. Based on these standards and cost adjustments, the average national gap between per-pupil funding in the highest-poverty and lowest-poverty districts is between $1,000 and $1,250 in cost-adjusted dollars. The racial implications are also dramatic, with the average gap between districts with the highest percentage of students of color and the lowest percentage of such students slightly higher than $1,000, and with gaps persisting in thirty-seven states.[27] Gaps of $1,000 per pupil per year, in a class of thirty students, would mean that schools with low-income kids of color would have, on average, an entire $30,000 less in resources per classroom than their whiter and wealthier suburban counterparts.

Among the reasons for these gaps is the way in which school funding is collected. Because of the emphasis on local funding of primary and secondary schools, and the reliance on property taxes to generate those funds in most states, poorer districts will lose out relative to wealthier districts, a configuration with both class and race consequences, given the disproportionate presence of persons of color among the poor. In Texas, for example, schools in rich communities receive five times as much, per pupil, as schools in poor communities, and per-pupil spending in New York City is only half as generous as in many of the surrounding suburban school districts of New York State.[28] On average, schools in wealthy districts receive about twenty-five percent more funding, per pupil, than typical schools in poor districts.[29]

The most pernicious aspect of funding schools with property tax revenue is that, as a result, poor areas often are forced to tax themselves at far higher rates than wealthier districts, in an attempt to come up with comparable revenue. Not only does such excessive taxation at the local level further deplete the marginal economic resources of lower-income persons, but it rarely succeeds in providing anywhere near equitable resources vis-à-vis more affluent schools. In the 1990s, poor districts in thirty-five states assessed higher property taxes than wealthy districts; yet those with the higher property values to begin with invariably ended up with more funds. In Illinois, for example, local property taxes are forty-three percent higher on average in poor communities than in wealthy ones.[30]

These resource disparities have a number of profound consequences. On the one hand, they make it harder to recruit top-notch teachers to schools that are in lower-income communities, especially since poor districts pay their teachers, on average, almost thirty percent less than wealthier districts.[31] As a result, students attending these poorer schools tend to be stuck with less-qualified, less-experienced teachers, much to the detriment of their educational achievement. For example, in schools that serve mostly students of color, students have less than a fifty–fifty chance of ending up with a math or science teacher with a degree in the field or who is especially licensed to teach those subjects. Similarly, newly hired teachers at mostly black and brown schools are five times more likely to be unlicensed in the field they are teaching than are newly hired teachers in schools that are filled with mostly white students. Nationwide, minority students are half as likely as whites to be taught by the most highly qualified teachers and twice as likely as whites to be taught by the least-experienced teachers.[32] When the most highly qualified, trained, and experienced teachers mostly end up teaching the students in affluent communities, those students' preexisting advantages over lower-income students of color are simply reinforced, adding to already substantial race and class disparities in educational outcomes.[33]

Indeed, of all the factors affecting student performance, teacher quality may be one of the most significant. Research from Texas shows that school districts with students who score high in first and third grade on standardized math tests, but whose students are then burdened with less-prepared teachers, will invariably witness a rapid decline in student performance through high school. On the other hand, districts with low-scoring students in first and third grade, but whose students are then taught by highly prepared and trained teachers, will see their students steadily improve their performance, until, by eleventh grade, the slow-starting students have displaced the quick-starting students at the top of test distributions, and the students who showed such promise early will have declined in terms of performance to below the state average.[34]

Similar research in Tennessee has found that fifth graders who spend three years with less prepared and less effective teachers score more than fifty percentile points lower on achievement tests than those students who were taught by teachers with more experience and qualifications, as defined by their own grades in college, their major, their score on the teacher's certification exam, and their past academic track record.[35]

Unequal school funding also results in higher average class sizes in urban schools, which then negatively affects learning and achievement and results in substantial gaps in the supplies necessary to teach at an adequate level. Students in lower-income schools, who are predominantly of color, are faced regularly with supply shortages, thanks to fewer per pupil resources. While only sixteen percent of teachers in affluent, mostly white schools report that they lack necessary classroom supplies, nearly sixty percent of teachers in higher poverty, heavily black schools report such resource shortages.[36]

Although conservatives sometimes claim that money has little impact on the quality of education received,[37] it is hard to listen to such claims with a straight face. The persons who say this, for example, never skimp on the money they spend for their children, in keeping with the theory that money does not matter; they do not volunteer to pull their children out of expensive private schools, or to ditch the tutors to whom they pay good money in order to boost their children's achievement; they do not eschew expensive test preparation classes for their children, prior to the SAT, for example—instead they make sure their kids have all the advantages going into those testing situations and are willing to pay for those advantages. These are hardly the actions of people who honestly believe that "money does not matter." Similarly, few of the folks who insist that money does not matter will decide to send their children to the local, inexpensive community college or trade school, as opposed to the very expensive private and even public university, because they believe the quality of the education is the same. We know better, even if the right would like us to think otherwise.

Just because some schools and individual teachers have done amazing things with limited resources, which conservatives often claim to back up their argument about money not making much difference, this says nothing about whether or not finances matter to the quality of a child's education. As Gary Orfield, of the Harvard Civil Rights Project puts it, "This assumption is like deciding that if one science teacher could build his own computer out of spare parts, our science programs should assume that we can have good science without money for equipment."[38] Yet, the people who make these kinds of arguments are never the ones whose children attend the kinds of schools that have to go without. Indeed, they know their children would never have to attend such a school, because if there was even a remote possibility of such a thing happening, they would want to make sure those schools were fully stocked with the latest resources. In other words, the folks who say money does not matter, generally have money, so to them, it does not matter.

"ABILITY TRACKING" AS WHITE RACIAL PREFERENCE

Further contributing to the marginalization of students of color and the privileging of whites is the process of "tracking," which has been prevalent in most school systems for years. Ostensibly to provide the most advanced students with the most challenging material and less advanced students with material they are capable of learning, so-called ability tracking plays out in a blatantly racist and classist fashion, depriving capable students of color and poor students of all colors of challenging educational opportunities, while elevating whites to positions of academic dominance. Indeed, the history of tracking calls into question whether it was ever about ability, as opposed to a desire to maintain race and class inequality.

Such practices began in the early twentieth century, only after large influxes of immigrants (who were typically seen as inferior to their Anglo-Saxon counterparts) entered the country. Seeing education as a way to socialize immigrant children and to "Americanize them," it was only at this stage that compulsory schooling began to emerge. Yet, there was no desire to provide the same high-quality instruction to such children as was being provided to the children of the elite: after all, some would still be needed to do the "difficult, manual tasks" in Woodrow Wilson's formulation. As such, different tracks were established to sort out "undesirables" from the children of the ruling class.[39] Similarly, in the South, there was virtually no "ability tracking" until after 1971—the year that most southern states were finally forced to implement significant desegregation plans via busing, forcing the question whether its introduction was really about sorting on the basis of ability, as opposed to resegregating classes by seemingly fair and neutral means.[40]

Nationally, black students are only half as likely as whites to be placed in high-track English or math, and 2.4 times more likely than whites to be placed in remedial classes in these core subjects.[41] Even when blacks demonstrate equal ability with their white counterparts, they are far less likely to be placed in advanced classes. When kids from lower-income families, who are disproportionately of color, correctly answer all math questions on a standardized test, they are still less likely to be placed in advanced tracks than children from upper-income families who missed a fourth of the questions and are twenty-six percent less likely to be placed in advanced tracks than upper-income persons with the same perfect scores.[42] Even the president of the College Board has acknowledged that black eighth graders with test scores comparable to the scores of whites are disproportionately placed in remedial high school classes.[43] In this sense, not only are equally capable students of color disadvantaged, but whites who are no more capable than their black and brown counterparts are advantaged, privileged, and receive a de facto form of racial preference.

In addition to overt bias from counselors or teachers, a primary factor contributing to the disproportionate placement of blacks and Latino/as in low-level classes is the lack of advanced classes in the schools attended by such children. In other words, no matter how bright students of color might be, if advanced classes simply are not offered in their schools, there is little chance that they will be exposed to the more challenging materials. Nationwide, one-third of all classes offered in mostly white schools are honors or advanced placement, compared to only eleven percent of classes in schools that are made up mostly of students of color, and there are two to three times more honors and advanced placement (AP) courses per capita for white suburban schools than for lower-income schools of color.[44]

As a result of tracking black and brown students away from honors and AP classes, and the simple lack of AP availability at heavily black schools, white high school seniors are 3.5 times more likely to have taken at least one AP exam for college credit, which would signify that they are approximately that much more likely to be placed in an AP class to begin with.[45] Although blacks make up seventeen percent of the nation's public school population, they comprise less than five percent of students taking an AP exam annually.[46] In California, blacks and Latino/as are forty-five percent of the state's students but comprise only thirteen percent of those taking an AP exam.[47] As most students who take AP classes go on to take the exams associated with them, this would seem to indicate that an equally small share of students in such classes are African American or Latino/a.

This pernicious and racist tracking occurs despite studies showing that more than ninety percent of all students can master virtually any course material so long as the material is presented in a challenging way, using appropriate instructional techniques. Tracking, by assuming that few students can master challenging material, deprives many who are quite capable of the opportunity to develop to their full potential.[48] Interestingly, nations with which we often compare ourselves do not begin tracking nearly as early in the school system as is done in the United States. Japan, for example, does not begin to track students based on so-called ability until after their equivalent of the ninth grade, at a time when it is reasonable to argue that a student's interests have developed in one direction or another.[49]

Ultimately, tracking causes black students to receive unequal educational opportunities, in large part because of the low expectations of them held by teachers: perceptions that can easily become self-fulfilling prophecies. If teachers believe African Americans and Latinos are capable of less, they will be unlikely to expose them to challenging materials or to push them to achieve, thereby lowering those students' own self-confidence and preparedness and thereby furthering a cycle of lesser achievement relative to their white counterparts. Because only about one-quarter of schools allow significant parental or student input into tracking decisions, the awful truth is that the academic futures and levels of exposure for kids of color are quite literally in the hands of teachers and counselors who, as all available evidence indicates, are often guided by race and class stereotypes about ability.[50] When we then consider that teachers assigned to teach in low-track classes tend to be the least experienced, this means that important decisions about what students will and will not be exposed to are being made by the teachers who are least prepared to make those decisions, and that the students who most need a qualified instructor are the least likely to actually receive one.[51]

The impact of placement in a low track in school has been shown to be profound. A low track fosters reductions in student feelings concerning their own abilities and helps depress aspirations for the future among low-tracked students. Students tracked low tend to be less involved in extracurricular activities, and they are more likely to drop out, even after other factors that can cause these same results are controlled for.[52] Indeed, the impact of placement in a low track stigmatizes students of color as less capable and has consequences for student attitudes comparable to the consequences of forced attendance at a segregated school.[53]

Teachers of low-tracked students routinely admit their own low expectations of the students in their care. As Oakes notes, the most common goals that teachers set for such students are not related to advancing to a higher level, or mastery of material, but, rather, teaching them discipline, respect for authority, punctuality, to smile on the job, practice good hygiene, learn how to write a check, how to know just enough to hold down a job, how to be less outspoken, and how to become content with their lives. In other words, students tracked low—disproportionately students of color and the poor—are taught how to be subordinate to others, not encouraged to think for themselves or develop their own potential skills.[54]

Students in low-track classes also receive less instruction during the school day. Higher-track English classes spend, on average, fifteen percent more time on instruction while high-tracked math classes spend an average of twenty-two percent more time on instruction. In all, the average time difference comes to nearly forty hours less instruction per year for low-track students. High-track English teachers also assign three times more homework, on average, than their low-track counterparts, and high-track math teachers assign forty percent more homework than those teaching lower-track math.[55]

On the other hand, students in high-track classes tend to demonstrate much greater levels of academic efficacy, confidence in their abilities, and a greater desire to go on to college. In addition, because advanced classes often are graded differently, and allow students to receive up to a 5.0 (instead of a 4.0) for an A, a 4.0 (instead of a 3.0) for a B, and so forth, those with access to these classes can boost their grade-point averages relative to non-advanced track students, thereby making them more desirable in the eyes of college admissions officers. So in

California, for example, the affluent, mostly white students at Beverly Hills High would be in a far better position, when it comes time for college admissions, than an equally capable student in one of the 129 high schools in the state that offer no AP classes at all.[56]

WHITE TEACHERS, CLASSROOM CLIMATE, AND RACIAL PREFERENCE

Although we might hate to acknowledge it, teachers often have low expectations of their students, especially students of color who come from low- and moderate-income families. One study of New Orleans teachers (in a system that is almost entirely black) found that sixty percent of the teachers did not believe black males in their schools would go on to college.[57] Although they may be correct in this assumption, the fact that they have such low expectations about the students in their classes calls into question the extent to which they can really be expected to teach everyone equally and make the maximum effort to reach the children in their care each day.

Even more disturbing than the low expectations teachers often have for students of color, one survey actually found a remarkably high percentage (twenty-six percent) of high school science teachers, ninety-four percent of whom are white, saying that it was either "definitely true" or "probably true" that "some races are more intelligent than others."[58] Such a position is not only unscientific in the extreme, as it presumes races to be distinct biological entities, in total opposition to the findings of modern genetics, but it is also the textbook definition of racism. Although the survey did not ask which race or races these teachers perceived as either probably or definitely inferior, it stands to reason that they would not think this of whites, that never having been a common stereotype in this culture. As almost all science teachers in the United States are white, it is also doubtful that they believe their own group to be the inferior one.

CULTURAL DISTANCE AND CROSS-CULTURAL MISINTERPRETATION

But even if we assume there is very little overt bias or racism among teachers in U.S. schools, various forms of subtle bias may creep into the process of teaching, in ways that place students of color at a distinct disadvantage and provide preferences to whites. Cultural misinterpretation and cross-cultural incompetence, for example, are not only predictable within American classrooms, they are also highly disruptive to the mission of equal educational opportunity. It cannot be seen as unimportant that approximately eighty-six percent of all public school teachers in the United States are white, mostly middle class and above, and significantly separated in a cultural sense from large numbers of their students, nearly forty percent of whom are children of color.[59] Their experiences in life (and likely in their own schooling) have been nothing like those of lower-income black and Latino/a students; as such, they may not be able to read the behaviors or attitudes of children of color properly, thereby mistaking boredom for lack of interest or ambition, or mistaking certain boisterous behaviors as abnormally aggressive and dangerous, and deserving of punishment, merely because the behavior conflicts with their own idea of "normal."

Once teachers come to view students of color as problems to be managed, rather than young minds to be fed knowledge, those students will fall farther and farther behind while whites continue to move forward. Amanda Lewis describes how administrators at one of the schools she observed regularly ignored the minimal focus on academics that was evident in classes with large numbers of students of color, preferring instead that the teachers merely maintain order. This deemphasis on academics, itself the result of low expectations about the students' abilities, then contributes to the very academic problems that feed the low expectations: namely, these students, having been neglected in terms of their exposure to academic materials, then score low on tests, and withdraw mentally from academic pursuits.[60] Once the students have been given over to this kind of cycle of neglect and underachievement, they will naturally be less likely to attend college or obtain a good job. Meanwhile, whites, whose classes tend to focus on mastery of the material at hand, are privileged by this arrangement, as their relative status is elevated, when contrasted to the students of color who are controlled, rather than taught.

White students even receive preferential treatment when they exhibit boredom and indifference in the classroom. Studies have indicated, for example, that when whites exhibit inattention in the classroom, teachers typically take it as an indication that they are failing to make the classroom work interesting. In other words, white student apathy is seen as reflecting on the failures of the teacher, failures that require immediate attention and correction. On the other hand, black students exhibiting the same sense of indifference or boredom are often pigeonholed as suffering from some malady, such as attention deficit disorder, or some type of oppositional personality syndrome. In other words, black student apathy is seen as reflecting on the inherent or perhaps cultural flaws of the student, or perhaps his or her family. It is rarely if ever taken to indicate that the teaching methods of the teacher are flawed.[61]

Unless teachers understand and respond to the often different learning styles of students of color as opposed to whites, they will invariably underserve the former and privilege the latter. For example, if a disproportionate number of black students in a school are lower-income, they will likely experience a learning environment at home that is considerably louder and less formally "organized" than in more affluent homes, which are disproportionately white. Not only are lower-income residences typically in louder communities, but internally there may be a greater degree of what some would consider chaos than in more affluent spaces. With a constant exposure to multiple stimuli from an early age, many black students will come to adapt to that kind of environment and actually learn best in such a space, while someone who was used to a more isolated, calm, and quiet environment would find such a setting unnerving. As such, when teachers insist on only one style of classroom management—sitting still in rows of chairs, and not talking unless called on—they subtly reinforce the learning style of more privileged students to the detriment of those raised in different settings.[62]

Similarly, the cultural styles of interaction in black communities are often different from those in white communities, leading to further problems when white teachers attempt to teach African American students. So, for example, whereas black communities place a high value on "call and response" interaction, in which there is a constant give and take between speaker and listener, white style tends to be more linear, characterized by speaker and listener as separate dichotomous entities. The teacher, or preacher, or performer teaches, preaches, or performs, while the student, parishioner, or audience member passively listens and observes. For white teachers, the culturally normal interaction style of black students, including interjection in the middle of a lesson or discussion, may be viewed as evidence that the student is disruptive and disengaged from the formal learning process, when instead such behavior may indicate a high level of engagement and interest.[63] That black students from high-income families are forty-three percent more likely than their white counterparts to be held back a grade[64] raises the question of how much of the differential treatment may stem from cultural misinterpretation of verbal cues given off by blacks, as opposed to whites.

A classic example of cultural misinterpretation is provided by Amanda Lewis, who recalls the way in which a white teacher she observed responded to culturally appropriate and culture-specific behavior by a black student as aggressive and disruptive, even when it was not. She notes how a black child in a class she observed was punished for pumping his arms in the air, in a "raise-the-roof" motion, after getting an answer correct in a math game. Obviously, he was not trying to disrupt the class—he was engaged in a math game, for goodness' sake—but his teacher thought the celebration inappropriate and proceeded to remove him from the game altogether.[65]

UNEQUAL DISCIPLINE AND THE MISREADING OF DANGER

It is in the area of unequal discipline that white teachers so often discriminate, whether intentionally or not, against students of color, and end up providing yet another systemic advantage to whites. A plethora of evidence going back decades suggests that black students are consistently punished, suspended, and expelled disproportionately, both relative to their percentages of the school populations and relative to their actual share of school rule violations. In this way, students of color are denied the opportunity to receive an education at all, above and beyond the generally inferior one to which they are exposed via tracking and underfunding. As just one example, a recent analysis of Minnesota schools found massive disparities in punishment. Statewide, blacks represent six percent of student enrollment but are thirty-six percent of students suspended. Whites, at eighty-four percent of enrollment, represent only fifty-one percent of students suspended. On a per capita basis, the suspension rate for blacks statewide was ten times higher than the rate for whites and four times higher than the national average.[66]

On a national level, a recent report by researchers at the Indiana University Education Policy Center and the University of Nebraska notes that of the fifteen major studies that have examined the issue of whether or not black students are disproportionately singled out for school disciplinary action, fourteen conclude in the affirmative. The only study not to find statistically significant racial disparity in punishment was limited to a small sample of schools in Kansas, meaning that nationwide evidence of racially disparate school discipline was and is overwhelming.[67]

As these researchers' meta-analysis of existing data and their own original research indicated, black students are suspended on average at a rate that is two to three times higher than their white counterparts, even though they do not violate school rules anywhere near two to three times more often. For most types of violations, in fact, there is no significant difference between whites and blacks in terms of rates of infractions. Indeed, the most serious rule violations in school are disproportionately the work of whites, while blacks are mostly disciplined for vague, less serious, and extremely subjective offenses, like "disrespecting authority," excessive noise, or loitering.[68] According to data collected by the Centers for Disease Control, over the past decade there have been no statistically significant differences between whites and blacks when it comes to carrying weapons on school grounds, drinking alcohol, smoking marijuana at school, or possessing drugs on campus. When it comes to smoking cigarettes (one of the more common "serious" rule violations), over the past decade, whites, on average, have been more than twice as likely as blacks to smoke on school grounds.[69]

Perhaps most interesting, and surprising for many, is the fact that when it comes to acts of violence on school property, there are no consistently significant differences among urban, suburban, and rural schools in terms of levels of victimization.[70] What differences *do* exist indicate slightly higher victimization rates in suburban (mostly white) schools than in urban schools. In 2000, for example, suburban students were victimized at a rate that was nine percent higher than urban students for all crimes, and twenty-seven percent higher for violent crimes. Even rural school students are victimized at rates that are comparable to urban students.[71] Over a seven-year period from 1992 to 1999, suburban victimization rates were equal to urban victimization rates as well, indicating that there is simply no greater risk of violence in city schools than noncity schools, contrary to popular belief.[72] As such, the disproportionate rate of disciplinary actions handed down to students of color cannot be explained by virtue of higher rates of violent behavior or weapons possession, contrary to what many might otherwise assume.

Although the suspension of blacks at higher rates is often "justified" as the result of having higher referral rates by teachers (implying that blacks are suspended because of a more extensive overall record of discipline problems), this begs the question of how and why they received disproportionate referrals in the first place. And it is in the area of teacher referrals and reactions to perceived black behavioral problems where studies have found the greatest degree of bias.[73] Available evidence indicates that white teachers in particular, who are uncomfortable and unfamiliar with the communication styles of children of color, will often presume that black student behavior is disruptive or even threatening when it is not. They tend to "see" argumentative and disrespectful behavior in ways they would not if the perpetrator of the behavior were white.[74]

FORMAL COLOR BLINDNESS AND THE REINFORCING OF WHITE DOMINATION

Having said that, however, classroom culture and teacher styles are not only a problem when students are treated radically differently. Such teachers may also inadvertently reinforce racial and class inequalities in their classrooms by way of their steadfast commitment to formal "color blindness," which leads them to insist that they treat all children the same, that they "don't even notice color," and that "kids are kids." Although such an attitude may appear enlightened, in fact it ignores the reality that not all children *are* the same and, specifically, not all children have the same experiences, challenges, or obstacles to overcome in their lives.

If teachers, for example, treat their low-income students of color the way they would treat students who did not face racism regularly, who did not experience the same level of economic hardship as they often do, and whose parents had college educations and steady, high-paying employment, they would be treating those students unfairly because they would be ignoring the social context within which their low-income black students are trying to learn. They would not be educating the actual child, but rather, just a theoretical child, divorced from his or her social reality.

Only by understanding where a child is situated in the larger opportunity and experience structure can a teacher actually teach the child where he or she is, and challenge that child to reach new heights. If teachers, on the other hand, treat their kids of color as if they were white, or their poor kids as if they were affluent, they will not provide the additional support structures to those children—since additional support might not be needed in the more privileged homes—and will therefore shortchange students in need. For example, a recent study found that although less than a third of white students say a teacher's encouragement motivates them to work hard, about half of black students say such encouragement is crucial for them.[75] As such, if teachers teach to the norm of what white students seem to require in order to put forth maximum effort, they will fail to provide the proper encouragement to their black students. In this way, treating students the same would tragically underserve students of color and privilege the needs of whites in return.

LANGUAGE, "OTHERING," AND THE REINFORCEMENT OF WHITE DOMINATION

Besides the flawed language and concepts of color blindness, there are other problems with the language often used by educators, problems that further entrench racial preference for whites in a number of ways. Labels often attached to students of color, like "at-risk" or "special needs," imply that the problem with such students, in terms of their achievement, is a skill deficit, and that they need to be "fixed," or changed to fit in with the so-called norm. But this language mystifies the process by which students come to be "at-risk" in the first place, a process that is hardly independent of the race and class oppression to which their families have been subjected, not only in schools, but in the labor market, housing, and other arenas of daily life. After all, rarely do we hear educators discuss racism, even though it surely must be one of the risks to which such students are exposed. Further, we do not address the "special need" of tackling racism either. It is as if these structural conditions are off the radar screen entirely.

By obscuring the way that structural factors place kids at risk, the language of the educational establishment implies that their problems are theirs, or perhaps to be found in their families, but not the system itself. As such, white domination is once again protected and maintained because it fails to be interrogated. Additionally, because racism is not seen as part of the problem, few educators emphasize the need for dominant group members, meaning whites, to change, or to plug up their skill deficits, which might include the skill of working cooperatively with students of races different from theirs. White privilege is completely ignored, as with other terms often used to describe students of color, such as "less fortunate" or "underprivileged." Both of these terms are passive, and fail to note that anyone ever *does* anything oppressive or harmful to anyone. The phrases imply that someone can be down, without noting that by definition someone must then be *up*. After all, *under* and *less* are relative terms, but rarely do we hear their advantaged counterparts referred to as the *overprivileged*, for example.

The language of diversity likewise leaves the white norm in place, by suggesting that we should "celebrate difference," while never interrogating the center, the norm, and how it came to be the norm, and what power imbalances assure that it will remain the norm, while other narratives, other cultural traditions, remain in the periphery.

MAINSTREAM MULTICULTURALISM AS REINFORCEMENT OF WHITE DOMINATION

Related to the problems associated with the language of diversity, what passes for multicultural education is rarely designed to alter the existing power dynamics within a school or the larger school system. Although conservatives claim that schools have bent over backward to accommodate the concerns of nonwhite students, in terms of the introduction of multicultural curricula, for example, the fact is, most of what passes for multicultural education is so watered down and superficial that, if anything, it actually *reinforces* white privilege and further provides strength to the dominant group's perspectives. Typically, these efforts are short-lived (perhaps centered around a particular time of year, like Black History Month) and symbolic, as with the placement of posters of famous people of color around the room, which are often then removed at the end of a particular lesson. A comprehensive examination by historian James Loewen of the twelve most common textbooks used in American history classes nationwide likewise found that they overwhelmingly underrepresented people of color, in terms of their contributions to the nation's history, favoring instead traditional white-dominated narratives that stressed even the most irrelevant details of white leaders' lives, and thereby reinforced the common perceptions that American history has been mostly a history of white accomplishment.[76]

Most troubling, multicultural educational efforts and programs tend to define the problem in a way that preserves white institutional power and privilege, by focusing on our "ignorance" of other group's cultures, but rarely discussing the power imbalances between them. By developing what amounts to a cultural tourist-type model of multiculturalism, most of the programs implemented under this rubric not only fail to challenge the status quo, but if anything reinforce it, by making all nondominant perspectives and narratives seem trivial by comparison to the norm.[77] Multiculturalism becomes something students "do" to learn about the somewhat exotic "other," but rarely in a way to interrogate the norms that they take for granted. By not examining those norms, they are then reinforced, to the benefit of those whose experiences fall under the category of "normal," which will more often than not be white students.

But because so few teachers receive any kind of comprehensive training in multicultural educational methods, it is not surprising that they fail to utilize multiculturalism in a way that really equalizes the classroom environment. Only four in ten public school teachers received any professional development training in multicultural education in 2000, and, of those, seventy percent had fewer than nine hours.[78]

AVOIDING THE R WORD: IGNORING RACISM AS REINFORCEMENT OF WHITE DOMINATION

Because they receive so little training even in the arena of multiculturalism, it will come as no surprise that teachers will be even less prepared to address racism itself. And this failure to address racism—indeed, the cultivated tendency to ignore or downplay the role that race plays in the institution, or the possible conflicts that arise from time to time—further contributes to white privilege and the transmission of racial advantage to white students.

Often, teachers and administrators will avoid any discussions of race or racism, out of fear of creating conflict, or perhaps upsetting parents. But the result of such evasion is that the perspective of the dominant group, which tends to believe that everything is okay when it comes to race relations, is then reinforced. Then, if and when racial incidents occur, or complaints are raised about racism by students or parents of color, the schools can and often will assume that the problem has been "created" by those doing the complaining, never having examined the norms in the school from a nonwhite perspective. In this fashion, parents and students of color are further ostracized and marginalized, while whites are able to remain secure in their denials of any race problem at all at their schools. The psychological advantage of not having to think about race or racism and, indeed, being institutionally empowered to ignore such issues altogether, is no minor concern.[79]

Teachers are so quick to deny the existence of racial tensions at their schools that even in the face of blatant incidents, they will seek to redefine and reinterpret the events as nonracial, or perhaps just a matter of "kids being kids" and teasing or being cruel to one another. White teachers are also given to accusing students of color who complain about racism or racial mistreatment of "playing the race card," thereby privileging the white perspective that everything is okay, and that the only race problem in a given school is the tendency of people of color to exaggerate the extent to which they experience unequal treatment.[80]

What all of this adds up to is a litany of advantages, some large and some small, some material and some psychological, but all of which prepare white students, more so than persons of color, for the process of applying to and then attending college. Whether it is from greater academic preparation, pre-existing familial advantage, tracking, unequal discipline, or simply the fact that whites have by and large had their learning styles and needs catered to for twelve years, all aspects of the educational system transmit racial privilege for the dominant group.

It is against this backdrop that conservative critiques of affirmative action must be evaluated. Only by first seeing the ways in which whites are preferenced from the very beginnings of the nation's educational system can an honest assessment of so-called racial preferences for people of color be administered. Too often the discussion about these "preferences" lacks any of the above context, and is presented as if affirmative action were the only time race had entered into the distribution of opportunity with the nation's educational system. As we will see, not only are conservative claims regarding preferential treatment for people of color in college admission flawed, but indeed, in many ways the admissions process continues to provide a number of advantages to whites.

3

RESPONDING TO CRITICS OF AFFIRMATIVE ACTION

Now that we have established the many ways white students are favored over nonwhites throughout the years of primary and secondary schooling in this country, we can examine the way affirmative action for people of color does and *does not* operate in higher education. After all, we might acknowledge that the earlier years of school provide advantages to whites and still claim that affirmative action programs at the college and university level, as well as in law schools, medical schools, and graduate institutions, more than balance out those prior preferences. We might still claim that affirmative action in higher education amounts to unfair preference, even though the larger system of preference favors members of the dominant group.

Conservatives typically make five principal arguments in opposition to affirmative action in colleges and universities: first, that such efforts amount to reverse discrimination and bump whites from slots in schools that they would otherwise obtain, and to which they are rightly entitled; second, that affirmative action requires colleges to lower their admissions standards and admit students of color who are less qualified than whites and who are then unable to keep up with the work at colleges that are ultimately too difficult for them; third, that preferences result in stigma and a loss of self-esteem for those who benefit from them, causing them to doubt their own abilities; fourth, that affirmative action is not needed as evidenced by the way in which Asian Pacific Americans have succeeded in this country; and, fifth, that the reason for black underachievement is not discrimination or any form of injustice that requires affirmative action as a response, but rather persistent cultural defects within the black community itself, including an inadequate attachment to education as a life goal.

THE MYTH OF REVERSE DISCRIMINATION

Conservatives claim that people of color are taking college admission slots from more-qualified whites, thanks to affirmative action in higher education. This notion has made affirmative action in colleges even more controversial in some ways than similar programs in the job market. White parents, concerned that their children might be rejected from the college of their choice because of "quotas," have increasingly turned hostile to affirmative action plans for higher education, voting to end the practice altogether in California and Washington State in 1996 and 1998, respectively, in large measure because of concern over the practice in the two state college systems.

As a result of relentless right-wing propaganda against affirmative action, whites often assume they have been unfairly victimized by "reverse discrimination" even before obtaining any information that could either confirm or deny their assumptions. So, for example, Jennifer Gratz, a rejected white applicant to the University of Michigan (whose reverse discrimination claim was recently decided by the Supreme Court) admitted that as soon as she received her rejection letter her response was to sue the school, because she "knew" people who had gotten in ahead of her despite being less qualified.[1] How she knew this without having examined the full applicant files of those accepted ahead of her is a mystery, but as she explained, "I had a suspicion right at the beginning that I had been discriminated against."[2] White hysteria over so-called reverse discrimination has no doubt been stoked by the efforts of conservative think tanks and organizations, like the Center for Individual Rights (CIR). The center has not only represented students like Gratz in their challenges to campus affirmative action programs, but has even gone so far as to take out advertisements in college newspapers, essentially *soliciting* lawsuits against "racial prefer-ences" for people of color.[3]

Claims of white victimization have also emerged with regard to affirmative action in the ranks of faculty. In the mid-1990s, one of the instigators of an anti–affirmative action initiative in California told a tale of his own victimization at the hands of racial preferences. Tom Wood, a scarcely published academic, complained about being rejected for a faculty position at San Francisco State University, so the school could offer the job to a "less qualified" woman of color. But after a brief investigation Wood was forced to admit that he had not even applied for the job, and that he had no idea of the qualifications of the woman who ended up with the faculty slot. As it turns out, she had published books and several scholarly journal articles, and so by any objective notion of merit would have beaten Wood in the competition even had he applied for the position.[4]

That anyone could believe persons of color were receiving preference in terms of faculty hiring is amazing, given the actual breakdowns of who is teaching on American college campuses.

According to the available data, almost nine in ten faculty members in the United States are white, less than six percent are black, less than four percent are Asian, less than two percent are Latino/a, and only two-tenths of one percent are American Indian.[5] When we look only at full professors, as opposed to part-time instructors and associate professors, only three percent of tenured faculty members are black in the United States.[6] One survey of faculty in the Midwest found that persons of color are significantly underrepresented as faculty, relative to their availability in the qualified pool of potential applicants. The study, by the Midwestern Higher Education Commission, found that qualified African Americans are only forty percent as likely to be faculty as their white counterparts; qualified American Indians are only half as likely to be faculty as their white counterparts; and qualified Latino/as, though faring a bit better, are still only three-fourths as likely to be hired as faculty as their white counterparts.[7]

As for student admissions, affirmative action programs in colleges have a very small impact on white college applicants. Most students attend colleges with no real affirmative action to speak of, in that blacks and whites are admitted at equal rates and anyone meeting minimal requirements is accepted. It is only in the most elite colleges, attended by the top students, that affirmative action comes into play at all.[8] Only fifteen percent of college freshmen apply to the most selective schools, for example, and only ten percent end up attending those schools. In fact, only a third of freshmen attend a school in one of the top two tiers of selectivity, with the rest attending schools whose selectivity is so low that there is no way to make a claim of "preference" for anyone, least of all students of color. Within those top two tiers, the student enrollment for blacks and Latino/as averages only about six percent each, hardly enough to suggest that they are bumping large numbers of whites who would otherwise be admitted.[9]

Furthermore, even if all college affirmative action programs were eliminated, the average white applicant's chances of admission to a given school would improve only from 25 percent to about 26.2 percent. For whites who score between 1200 and 1249 on the SAT (an excellent score but somewhat borderline at the most selective colleges), eliminating affirmative action completely would only raise the odds of admission from nineteen percent to twenty-one percent; and for those scoring between 1250 and 1299 the odds of admission if all affirmative action programs were eliminated would only rise from twenty-three to twenty-four percent.[10]

Finally, even with so-called "preferences" for people of color, whites are more likely than any other racial or ethnic group to be admitted to their college of first choice, while blacks are *least* likely to be accepted to their first-choice school.[11] In fact, despite so-called favoritism shown to blacks under affirmative action, the rate at which colleges and universities have been admitting blacks has actually *fallen* since the 1970s.[12] At the most selective colleges and universities, increases in black student enrollment have continued to lag far behind such increases for all other racial groups, actually widening the gaps over the last several decades between blacks and others in terms of whether they will be enrolled at such top schools.[13]

In part, this tendency of whites to be favored in admissions may be related to subtle perceptual biases on the part of the mostly white admissions officers at selective colleges and universities. Experimental studies, for example, have found that whites will tend to favor other whites and disfavor blacks when evaluating their college applications, especially at the highest levels of qualifications. In other words, among highly qualified applicants (the kind who traditionally seek admission to elite schools), it may be whites who receive the benefit of more positive perceptions of their abilities, no matter the existence of affirmative action policies.[14]

Similarly, despite claims that colleges are falling all over themselves to recruit and admit students of color, the truth is that from 1992 to 2000, the share of schools that were actively recruiting people of color, with deliberate and targeted efforts (which is the most common and extensive form of affirmative action, typically, in higher education), fell from two-thirds of colleges to only fifty-one percent. Among four-year public institutions, such as large state schools, whereas ninety-one percent had been actively recruiting students of color in 1992, by 2000 only sixty-six percent were.[15]

Not only that, but at several schools white students are just as likely as students of color to benefit from programs intended to give preference to slightly less academically advanced students. A study of the UCLA Academic Advancement Program—aimed at students who are somewhat less prepared than others upon arrival at the college—found that the percentages of students of color admitted through "special admissions" (meaning they were accepted despite not technically meeting the normal requirements for admission) were roughly identical to the percentages of whites accepted through the same special admissions program.[16]

As for the area of college scholarships—another arena in which some complain students of color receive preference via scholarships that are set aside for blacks, for example—there is no evidence that these scholarships crowd out money available to whites. According to a report by the General Accounting Office in 1994, only one-quarter of one percent of all undergraduate scholarship money comes from scholarships that are restricted to people of color (and even these are privately funded), and even counting scholarships where race is among the many factors considered, less than four percent of scholarship money given out nationwide would be represented by these awards.[17] Likewise, only about 3.5 percent of students of color in the country receive race-based scholarships for college.[18]

A final problem with the claim that affirmative action amounts to reverse discrimination was outlined by the late political science professor Ronald J. Fiscus in his 1992 book, *The Constitutional Logic of Affirmative Action*. As Fiscus explains, unless one believes in the inherent inferiority of blacks, for example, one would have to assume that in the absence of institutional racism and white privilege, historically speaking, blacks would be roughly equally distributed throughout the economy and educational institutions, relative to their share of the population. There would be no reason to believe that they would not have obtained the same average qualifications, grades, test scores, or other credentials as whites. In the job market, there would be no reason to expect blacks *not* to be roughly the same share of doctors, lawyers, engineers, or whatever else as their share of the population—now between twelve and thirteen percent. Unless one believes blacks to be less capable of succeeding in these professions or in school, the only rational assumption to make is that the difference between the share of blacks at a given college, or in a given job, and their share of the population indicates the effect of discrimination past and present on black opportunity.

That said, any policy such as affirmative action, which boosts the representation of blacks at a given educational institution, cannot, by definition, be seen as an unfair racial preference, because, in the absence of the prior inequality of opportunity, blacks would have obtained all the necessary qualifications to attend those schools anyway. Likewise, those whites currently "burdened" by affirmative action would not have been in a position of superior qualifications to obtain those slots that they are now being "denied." Fiscus makes this argument explicit in his discussion of the landmark *Bakke* case, in which white applicant Alan Bakke sued the medical school of the University of California, Davis, because of its admissions policy, which set aside 16 of 100 slots in the first-year class for racial minorities. Bakke won his case, although Fiscus explains why the reasoning behind his "reverse discrimination" argument was fundamentally flawed:

> In a more perfect world those minority applicants *would* have achieved superior high school records and MCAT scores *in proportion to their percentage of the general population*. And in that more perfect world, Bakke's so-called objective record *would have placed him below the top 100 candidates*. Bakke apparently would have ranked among the top hundred *white* applicants, but he would not have ranked among the top hundred of *all* candidates. To reward Bakke by admitting him instead of a minority candidate was to allow him to reap one of the rewards of society's racism.... Bakke had no right to that seat in the first year class because in the absence of racism it would have been fairly won by a minority applicant.... There is no violation of equal protection when society acts to restore the equilibrium that would have naturally occurred under non-racist conditions.[19]

In other words, affirmative action, even if implemented as proportional quotas (which is not the policy at any college or university in the United States), would not necessarily violate any rights to which whites could reasonably lay claim or to which they are otherwise entitled. After all, in the absence of prior racism (to say nothing of ongoing racism in the present), unless we assume that blacks are inferior as a group, we would expect that blacks would have obtained slots in colleges in rough proportion to their numbers in the population of potential applicants. As such, the only "right" obviated by affirmative action, even in quota form, would be the "right" of whites to continue reaping the benefits of the previous injustice—but that is not a right that whites have to begin with.

In Bakke's case, the argument put forth by Fiscus is especially apt. After all, Bakke had attended school in Dade County, Florida, whose school system had been found by a federal court to have illegally segregated students during the years Bakke was there. Therefore, Bakke had directly reaped the benefits of prior white preference in education, calling further into question how "entitled" he would be to any slot in any college or medical school, relative to people of color.[20]

Speaking of Bakke, a careful examination of his personal tale of reverse discrimination renders specious his claim to have been a victim even in theory. First, Bakke was thirty-seven years old when he applied, and may well have been rejected because of his age, not race; thirty-seven is far older than the norm for persons applying to medical school. Second, Bakke was rejected at ten other schools, one of which had no minority set-asides and three of which had fewer than five percent applicants of color. Also, the year Bakke was rejected, eighty-four whites were admitted, thirty-six of whom had lower entrance exam scores than his own. Yet Bakke never complained that these "less qualified" whites were admitted ahead of him. And finally, all but one of the blacks admitted to Davis ahead of Bakke went on to graduate, indicating they too were qualified, despite lower MCAT scores.[21] In fact, during the history of the "special admissions" program for minority students at UC Davis, black students admitted under the program had graduated at a rate greater than ninety percent, indicating they were far from unqualified as medical school students.[22]

Additionally, the head of the admissions committee who personally interviewed Bakke found him to be "limited" in his approach to medicine and deeply committed to his personal views about the profession, as opposed to taking a more thorough and open-minded approach. Even without the affirmative action plan at UC Davis, Bakke's chances of admission would have improved only marginally, from sixteen to nineteen percent, and indeed in the two years that he applied, he never even made the wait list—evidence that race was not the deciding factor helping to advance others over him.[23]

Deep down, it appears that whites know how flawed their claims of reverse discrimination really are, and how much more beneficial it is to be white. Consider what happened in Riverside, California when school officials proposed naming the town's new high school for Martin Luther King, Jr. Despite the near secular sainthood claimed for King by many, and the extent to which the nation has ostensibly embraced his civil rights vision, white parents in Riverside objected strenuously to the attempt to name their children's school for King. When asked, most expressed concern that the name might signal to colleges that the school was in a black neighborhood, and thus not as competitive an institution.[24] Such a fear indicates just how aware whites really are about their privileges and advantages, and how much they seek to maintain them over people of color. After all, if affirmative action programs really were tantamount to racial preference for blacks, white parents would seemingly *want* college officials to think their children were black or that they lived in an "underprivileged" community, thereby making them eligible for some form of compensatory preference. To the extent whites fear being thought of as black, or tainted by blackness, they not only signal a recognition that reverse discrimination is a nonissue, but more to the point they clearly recognize the ongoing benefits that they and their children obtain by virtue of being thought of as white, and ultimately of *being* white.

Case Study 1:
"Reverse Discrimination" at the University of Michigan

As with the general claims of reverse discrimination made by opponents of affirmative action, the narrative of white victimization played a prominent role in the recent legal challenges to the University of Michigan's affirmative action plans. In June 2003, the Supreme Court ruled in two cases from Michigan, one involving the undergraduate school of Literature, Sciences, and the Arts and the other involving the University of Michigan Law School. In the undergraduate case, the Court struck down the affirmative action policy, calling it an unconstitutional racial preference system, but in the law school case, it upheld affirmative action, saying that the way in which the law school evaluated applicants was less preferential than in the undergraduate institution.

Although the cases are now decided, it is worth examining the facts of each, especially considering the likely future attempts by conservatives to attack even those kinds of policies that the Court left in place with its ruling. What's more, the ruling in the undergraduate case exhibited a gross failure by the Court to understand the validity of so-called racial preferences, thus, the need to examine the facts herein.

Consider the case against the university's undergraduate College of Literature, Sciences, and the Arts. According to the plaintiffs, and ultimately the majority of the Supreme Court, white applicants were at an unfair disadvantage because the university awarded twenty points (out of a possible 150-point evaluation scale) to students who come from "underrepresented minority" groups (or URMs for short), which are defined by the school as African Americans, Latino/as, and American Indians. Because these were twenty points that were, by definition, off-limits to whites, critics contended that the policy was ipso facto a form of racial "preference" and unfair discrimination.

Yet such a simplistic reading of the Michigan program was misleading for a number of reasons. First, there was no dispute by the white plaintiffs that each and every applicant of color admitted to the university was fully qualified to be there.[25] Additionally, there was no dispute that the same year the lead plaintiff in the case was rejected by the University of Michigan, there were fourteen hundred other non-URMs (mostly whites) who were admitted despite having lower test scores and grades than she did. And there were two thousand other non-URMs rejected who had higher grades and test scores than she.[26] The first of these facts proves that whites were not being rejected to make way for "less qualified" people of color, as they were actually getting passed over mostly for other whites, including those less "qualified" than themselves. The second of these facts demonstrates that the lead plaintiff in this case, whose claim for reverse discrimination was presumably strongest, would not have likely gotten into the University of Michigan, even if there had been no affirmative action programs. As the data show, there were at least two thousand other whites and Asians ahead of her in line, if test scores and grades had been the sole or primary factors, as affirmative action critics seem to prefer.

Furthermore, a careful examination of the point system reveals that it hardly operated as an antiwhite tool for discrimination. Of all the points available to applicants, the single most important factor was the last two years of high school grades, worth eighty points in all. There was also a maximum of twelve points available for SAT score. Although some critics of affirmative action pointed to this fact as proof of the system's unfairness—as having a perfect SAT would get an applicant eight fewer points than being black, for example—the school's decision in this regard was based on the hard data that indicate grade-point average is by far the most relevant indicator of likely success in college, and that adding SAT score to the mix only marginally increases the chances of selecting successful students.[27]

It should also be noted that although URMs could get twenty points that whites could not get, applicants from low-income backgrounds, *regardless of race*, and applicants who attended low-resource schools, *regardless of race*, would also have twenty points added to their totals. Because these three twenty-point "bonuses" could not be combined with one another (in other words, poor blacks from inner city schools were not getting sixty points), the effect of such a policy was to provide the same twenty points to disadvantaged whites and Asians as were provided to blacks, Latino/as, and American Indian students.[28]

Additionally, there were many other points that were available to whites, and which it would have been very unlikely for URMs to receive. For example, applicants from the state's Upper Peninsula—a rural, more isolated, and overwhelmingly white area—received sixteen additional points: ten for simply being from Michigan, and another six for being from that particular part of Michigan.[29] Since the Peninsula is overwhelmingly white, applicants from that region who were poor, for example, could receive twenty points for their economic status and sixteen for hailing from the Upper Peninsula, while a black, Latino/a, or American Indian applicant who was poor and from Chicago (as many applicants to the school are) would only get the twenty points for race. Even a poor black applicant from Detroit would be at a disadvantage compared to the poor white applicant from the Upper Peninsula; the former would get twenty points for race and ten for in-state residence, for a total of thirty; but the poor Upper Peninsula applicant would receive twenty, plus ten, plus six, for a total of thirty-six.

Also, the University of Michigan awarded up to ten points for attending an academically challenging high school, and eight more for taking an especially demanding curriculum.[30] But because of the interrelationship of race and economic status, people of color are disproportionately underrepresented at the most affluent and challenging private and public schools—indeed, blacks comprise only six percent of students at the nation's most affluent, and often most challenging, schools, while whites are eighty-four percent of students in these schools[31]—and as mentioned in a previous section, are about a third as likely to be placed in advanced or honors classes as their white counterparts. Thus, through no fault of their own, black, Latino/a, and American Indian students were all but excluded from access to these eighteen points, while whites would be disproportionately likely to receive them.

The University of Michigan also awarded four points to applicants whose parent or grandparent attended the school—a benefit that would almost all go to whites, given the history of segregation in higher education and American society generally—as well as up to twenty points for athletic ability, five for "leadership and service," three for a personal essay, and an additional twenty at the provost's discretion for students with some special quality not covered by the previous criteria.[32]

What all of these different factors make clear is that the whites who successfully sued the University of Michigan were not likely bumped to make way for people of color, so much as to make way for other whites who fit certain criteria better than they did. In the case of undergrad plaintiff Jennifer Gratz, she missed out not merely on the twenty points awarded to URMs but also the six points given to Upper Peninsula applicants (above and beyond the ten she received as an in-state resident from a Detroit suburb), the twenty points given to low-income students including whites, the four points given to children of alumni, and the points given to persons with special athletic ability.[33] And of course, Gratz had no complaint about receiving ten preference points for being an in-state student, even though such a preference would indeed put perhaps more-qualified applicants from out of state at a disadvantage.

Ultimately, none of the plaintiffs in this case ever showed in court (nor did they even try to show) that they would have been admitted in the absence of affirmative action. Indeed, there were far more points that were likely to be disproportionately awarded to whites, and that were all but off-limits to people of color, than there were points available to people of color that were off-limits to whites.

Case Study 2:
"Reverse Discrimination" at Michigan Law School

In the law school case, the so-called "proof" of racial preference and "reverse discrimination" offered by the plaintiffs' experts was even more contentious than at the undergraduate level, and this is likely why the Court voted to sustain the law school policy. Even though the matter is now settled law, it would be advisable to review the facts of the case, if for no other reason than to defend against the likely conservative attacks that will now pour forth, criticizing the Court for allowing the law school's type of affirmative action program to remain in place.

As it turns out, unlike the undergraduate level, there has never been a point system that awards points to URMs at the law school. As such, those who sought to eliminate the program at that level had to change their approach and their arguments. By utilizing questionable statistical techniques, plaintiffs claimed that black applicants to the University of Michigan Law School, in particular, were receiving preference over whites because they were being accepted with grade-point averages and LSAT scores that for whites were met with rejection. According to these experts, the odds of a black applicant being admitted to University of Michigan Law School were often hundreds of times better than the odds of a white applicant with similar scores and grades. Although the plaintiffs never presented evidence that the blacks admitted were unqualified—and indeed they conceded that every black student admitted had been fully qualified for admission—they insisted that when blacks and whites had equal qualifications, the blacks were more likely to be accepted, thereby indicating a preference.

In the University of Michigan case, the plaintiffs presented grid displays that broke down those students who applied and were admitted to the law school by "qualification cells"—basically separating students into groups by grade-point average and

LSAT (for example, a 3.5 to 3.75 GPA and 156 to 158 on the LSAT, on a scale of 120 to 180). For each cell, statistician Kinley Larntz calculated the odds of admission for a student in that cell, by race. His conclusion was that blacks in many of the cells had much greater chances of admission than whites in the same cells with the same grade and test score qualifications.[34] He then calculated the odds ratios for each cell. In other words, if blacks in a given cell had a fifty percent chance of admission and whites had a twenty-five percent chance of admission, the odds ratio would be 2:1. The larger the odds ratio, the greater the degree of presumed preference.

But such an analysis was terribly flawed. First, as even Larntz admitted, the data used to calculate relative admissions odds ratios were limited. In fact, any time blacks and whites in a given "qualification cell" were treated the same—either all accepted or all rejected—Larntz simply threw out their data and refused to consider it. In other words, by only examining cells where there was some level of differential outcome, Larntz automatically guaranteed and inflated the size of that difference. Overall, forty percent of the minority students who applied to the University of Michigan Law School were in qualification cells that exhibited no difference in admission odds ratios between whites and blacks, meaning his claims of massive differential treatment, and preference for blacks, depended on ignoring forty percent of all applicants of color to the law school.[35]

Second, Larntz's creation of the grid squares was entirely random and without statistical validity. His decision to limit the range of LSAT scores in each grid square to three points per square, while utilizing a GPA range of less than four-tenths of a point (3.5 to 3.75, for example, and 156 to 158 or 160 to 162) was entirely illegitimate, as even the developers of the LSAT admit score ranges of *seven points* between students can be entirely random and meaningless in terms of indicating actual ability.[36]

This problem with the LSAT is discussed in more detail in the following section, but for now suffice it to say that by simply flattening out the ranges in Larntz's grids to consider the random range of scores acknowledged by the Law School Admissions Council (LSAC), the magnitude of the so-called racial preference extended to URMs at Michigan all but evaporates.[37]

Second, differential odds ratios for white and black acceptance to the law school could just as easily have resulted from a system that involved zero racial preference for blacks, as from a system with large preferences for blacks. The different odds ratios resulted in large part automatically from the small sample sizes of applicants of color. For example, in 1996, among the "most qualified" applicants (students with a 3.75 GPA or better and a 170 or higher on the LSAT), only one black with these numbers applied to the University of Michigan and was accepted; 151 whites applied with these numbers, of whom 143 were accepted.[38] While almost everyone at this level was admitted to the school, since there was only one black who applied and got in, the "odds ratio" in favor of blacks at that level appears to be infinite—a guarantee for blacks and a slightly less than certain probability for whites. But surely one cannot infer from one accepted black out of one black applicant at that level that there was some pattern of preference operating.

As proof that one could produce odds ratios favoring blacks even in the absence of racial preference for any individual black applicant, consider the implications of a recent study by the Mellon Foundation and the Education Policy Center of the Urban Institute. According to the study, blacks tend to have faced greater educational obstacles than whites with comparable scores on standardized tests. When compared to whites with scores comparable to their own, blacks in a particular range are far more likely to have come from low-income families and families with less educational background. These black students are also more likely to have attended resource-poor inner city schools where educational opportunities are more limited than the mostly suburban schools attended by whites. Thus, black students can be said to have overcome more and be more "qualified" than whites who score in the same range or even a bit higher on standardized tests.[39]

As such, it becomes easy to see how students of color might end up with higher admissions odds at a given score level, even without any individual case of preference. Simply put, if whites as a group tend to be better off and face fewer obstacles to their educational success than blacks, and if blacks as a group tend to be worse off and face more obstacles, then black applicants to a college, law school, or graduate school will likely have a greater claim for their merit at a given test score level than whites who scored the same. To visualize the point, imagine a four-leg relay race. If whites as a group tend to start out two laps ahead of blacks (or even one lap, or half a lap) and after the race is run, the runners end up in a tie, is it really fair to say they were equally good as runners; or would we instead say that the black runner was superior, having made up so much ground?

Because even the plaintiffs in the case agreed there was nothing wrong with considering the obstacles faced by applicants—including racism and the effects of racism on academic performance—it is quite possible that admissions officers could simply look at applicant files, see whites and blacks with comparable scores, and then on an individual basis make the determination that the applicants of color (based on information in their files that was unavailable to Larntz) were more qualified, having overcome obstacles faced by far fewer whites. But if such individual and nonpreferential analyses were completed with such a result, they would still have produced the same odds ratios discovered by Larntz. In other words, differential odds ratios themselves prove nothing.

Indeed, the implications of accepting differential odds ratios as evidence of "reverse discrimination" would have been chilling, and it is vital that such arguments not be allowed to prevail in future legal challenges to affirmative action. In practice, such analyses would require the rejection of almost all applicants of color to selective schools, simply because there are so few applicants of color, especially at the upper levels of LSAT scores. Because of the small pool of applicants of color, for a school to then accept one out of one or two out of two would require that all whites in that range also be admitted (irrespective of individual analysis of their files), or that blacks be accepted in the same proportion as whites. But this latter option might not be possible when the number of blacks in the range is small.

For example, imagine a situation where there were one hundred white applicants to the University of Michigan Law School with a 3.3 GPA and 160 or higher on the LSAT. If the school accepted nine of these applicants, the white probability of admission at that level would be nine percent. But let us say that there were only nine applicants to the school who were black and scored in that range. To accept even one of those nine would be illegitimate under an odds ratio analysis, while to accept two or three would be viewed as massive preference, simply because it would mean a higher acceptance probability at that level than for whites. In effect, such a reliance on odds ratios punishes minorities for being minorities.

To further make the point, imagine an applicant pool where there are only one or two black applicants for each "qualification cell," perhaps because the school is in a very white location and does not typically attract applications from black students. Under an odds ratio analysis that said blacks could not have more favorable odds of admission without this serving as proof of reverse discrimination, most of those blacks, no matter how competent, would have to be rejected simply because to accept one out of one or two out of two would represent "infinite odds" and require the acceptance of every white in the same cell, merely to keep the odds ratios the same. So although we could expect the whites and blacks at the lowest level of scores to all be rejected and those at the top to all possibly be accepted, in the middle such a situation would create total chaos. If one black applied with scores and grades that were high but not necessarily a sure thing for admission, and two hundred whites applied with those same numbers, the school would have to accept every white in that cell if they accepted the one black, or else face a lawsuit for reverse discrimination on the basis of an unacceptably pro-black admissions odds ratio.

Moving beyond mere hypotheticals, there is real evidence of how reliance on odds ratios would work in practice. In 1996, for example, there were only two black students in the entire country who received LSATs over 170 and had GPAs of 3.75 or better.[40] If one of these applied to a given law school, that person would have to be rejected—under an odds ratio analysis—unless the law school was ready to accept every white applicant with that same score and GPA, irrespective of other aspects of their application file. Now imagine that the same year, one hundred whites with those numbers applied to the same school, and eighty of them were admitted, or ninety, or ninety-five; and imagine that both of the blacks with those grades and scores applied. Because admitting both of the blacks would yield odds ratios unacceptably large and in favor of blacks, the school would have to reject one of the blacks with those numbers (thereby producing an even larger odds ratio in favor of whites) just to avoid being sued for reverse discrimination!

Even the strongest evidence presented by Larntz to "prove" racial preference for blacks at University of Michigan indicated the problem with utilizing odds ratio analyses. Larntz noted, for example, that among applicants in 1999 with a 3.5 to 3.75 GPA and LSATs of 156 to 158, six of seven applicants who were "underrepresented minorities" were admitted, while only one of seventy-three whites at that level was accepted. This yielded an odds ratio of 432:1 in favor of URMs at that level, a seemingly huge racial preference.[41] But there are two apparent problems.

First, with only seven black, Latino/a, or American Indian applicants to the University of Michigan Law School in that particular "qualification cell," it was entirely possible, and even likely, that the admissions officers who decided to accept six of those seven merely examined the files closely and found that those six had overcome extraordinary obstacles (including racism and its consequences, not to mention economic hardship), unlike the white applicants. Thus, the ratio itself, absent other supporting evidence about the particular decision making of admissions officers, cannot automatically prove a racial preference for URMs. A claim of preference might be tenable if dozens of applicants of color with these borderline scores and grades had been accepted, while only one white in that range had, but with such a small pool involved, such a claim simply cannot be sustained.

Second, to have balanced out the odds ratios for this particular qualification cell, given the much smaller pool of people of color at that level, Michigan would have been forced into an untenable position. If we assume that seven of eighty applicants with that combination of test scores and grades was worthy of acceptance (essentially what the university was saying that year), this yields an acceptance probability at that level of 8.75 percent. Applying that acceptance probability to each group yields six whites of seventy-three who should be accepted and 0.6 URMs of seven who should be accepted. In other words, because of the small pool of URMs in that group, it would not have been possible to admit even one of them, let alone one black, one Latino/a, and one American Indian, without giving a slightly higher probability of admission to URMs as a group.

But let us say the school went ahead and rounded up the six-tenths of a person to one full person and admitted one URM with the above-mentioned numbers. Thus, instead of six URMs admitted with those numbers (the result for 1999) and one white admitted with those numbers, we would have had the opposite: six whites and one URM. The problem is that even with that "correction" the probability of acceptance for URMs at that level would be fourteen percent, while for whites it would be 8.2 percent, meaning that there would still be an unacceptable odds ratio favoring people of color, simply as a function of small sample size. In short, even under a "race-blind" process that was based on avoiding differential odds or substantially different probabilities for different groups, it would have been—and would be in the future—virtually impossible to completely eliminate favorable odds ratios for people of color.

As one final point regarding Michigan and the law school case, for each of the years under contention in the lawsuit, white applicants to the University of Michigan Law School had a higher rate of acceptance than black applicants. For example, in 1997, thirty-four percent of black applicants were admitted to the law school while thirty-nine percent of white applicants were admitted. In 2000, thirty-six percent of black applicants were admitted, while forty-one percent of white applicants were.[42] What's more, there were hundreds of whites involved in this lawsuit, all claiming to have been victimized by the University of Michigan policies—this, despite that in the years covered by the lawsuit there were only a few dozen people of color admitted to the law school at all, with or without the help of affirmative action.[43] In other words, it is simply impossible to believe that the majority of the whites in this case would have been admitted, even if Michigan had not operated an affirmative action plan.

THE MYTH OF LOWERED STANDARDS AND UNQUALIFIED PEOPLE OF COLOR

Ultimately, however, it is not enough to demonstrate that the real impact of affirmative action on whites is small, or that statistical evidence of racial preference for blacks and Latino/as at a given school is faulty. It is also vital to point out that people of color admitted to colleges that utilize affirmative action are not less qualified than whites under any rational analysis. Despite claims to the contrary, those students of color are qualified for the opportunities they receive. Information from the University of Michigan illustrates the point. Blacks admitted to the University of Michigan Law School from 1995 to 2000 had college GPAs that were equal to or better than their white counterparts. In fact, the lowest GPA of any black student admitted was higher than that of many whites admitted. Similarly, all of the Mexican-American students admitted had GPAs above several of the white students admitted.[44]

The right is quick to argue that students of color being admitted to the University of California system prior to the 1995 decision by the system's regents to ban affirmative action in admissions had been less qualified. As evidence, they cite the falloff in black and Latino/a admissions after the ban went into effect. But the year after the ban went into effect—the same year that voters imposed a statewide ban on affirmative action under Proposition 209—the top University of California schools blocked the admission of more than eight hundred blacks and Latino/as with 4.0 GPAs and 1200 or better (on a 1600 scale) on their SATs, who were clearly qualified under most anyone's interpretation of the term.[45]

Likewise, in 2003 University of California Regent John Moores released information purporting to demonstrate ongoing racial preference at Berkeley and UCLA despite the ban on such preferences in 1995. Yet the report, which noted that in 2002 there had been 781 students admitted to those schools with SATs below 1000, and some 4900 rejected despite SATs of 1400 or above, was terribly flawed for several reasons. First, those admitted and rejected were not classified by race, so there was no way to know how many of the low SAT scores were turned in by people of color. Second, half of those admitted with SATs below 1000 had been in the top four percent of their graduating classes, which means they are automatically eligible for admission due to high performance in high school, while the other half had almost unanimously demonstrated other talents or abilities that were considered important, including athletic ability. Third, almost all of those with SATs above 1400 who were "rejected" had withdrawn their applications, or had applied to the much more competitive engineering program, or were out-of-state, in which case standards are always set higher so as to prefer students from the State of California. In other words, the data that critics of affirmative action rely upon to demonstrate unfair preferential treatment demonstrate nothing of the sort. Considering that SAT scores have almost no independent correlation with grades at Berkeley (above and beyond what high school grades alone can predict), it is especially absurd to claim admissions policies there result in truly lowered standards or the sacrifice of academic quality.[46]

According to right-wing critics of affirmative action there are two principal "proofs" that affirmative action beneficiaries are less qualified for admission to top colleges than whites: the first is that blacks, especially, have far lower scores than whites on standardized tests such as the SAT, GRE, MCAT, and LSAT; the second is that graduation rates for these students of color are also far below the rates for whites, indicating that, once admitted to selective schools, blacks were largely in "over their heads." Let us examine these separately, although the arguments are largely related to one another.

The Fallacy of "Meritocracy": Debunking the SAT and Standardized Tests

Critics of affirmative action point to the persistent racial gaps on tests like the SAT as confirmation that blacks are admitted to selective schools via racial preference, despite that they are less qualified for slots in these schools than whites and Asians. But while it is true that these racial score gaps are real, this is not even remotely enough to prove that beneficiaries of affirmative action are truly less capable than others as students.

First, it is often argued that since whites at most schools have higher average SAT scores than blacks at the same schools, blacks admitted must have received preference. For example, in their report on "racial preferences" at the nation's military service academies—West Point and the Naval Academy—the Center for Equal Opportunity notes as its primary proof of unfair preference, the fact that whites at West Point have a median SAT score one hundred points higher than the median score for blacks. Likewise, they note that whites at the Naval Academy, in Annapolis, Maryland, have a median SAT that is 150 points above the black median.[47]

But to argue that racial score gaps between students attending a given school prove there was a preference given to blacks at the point of admission is demonstrably absurd and the height of statistical illiteracy. Since the average black score generally on the SAT is lower than the average white score (for reasons to be examined below), this means there will be "average" score gaps at most all schools; but that hardly means that any individual student had standards lowered for him or her. If there are fewer black and more white applicants to a given school with very high SAT scores, the averages of those admitted will reflect a racial gap even if every applicant were admitted in rank order based on SAT.[48]

Second, the claim that SAT score is indicative of merit is also flawed on an individual level. Much as with IQ scores, the SAT is an inadequate indicator of ability in school, let alone later in professional life, and is known to underpredict black college graduation rates.[49] In fact, SAT gaps of as many as three hundred points between two students or groups can be completely insignificant in terms of indicating actual ability differences.[50] Furthermore, individual score swings of sixty to sixty-five points (and therefore gaps between any two test takers of 120 to 130 points) are considered random by the test makers themselves and say nothing about the different abilities of the students in question.[51] Because missing only a few questions can result in wide scoring differences between test takers, for schools to base admissions decisions on SAT scores seems particularly ludicrous.[52]

Among other problems, results on the SAT are heavily influenced by test preparation classes (more available to those with money),[53] and recent evidence of widespread cheating on the test by white suburbanites calls into question the validity of test results.[54] In fact, given the correlation between SAT score and family income, its continued emphasis in admissions harms not only students of color but also poor and working-class white applicants, relative to their more affluent competitors. Studies have shown that for every $10,000 less that a student's family earns relative to another student's family, that first student will, on average, receive fifteen fewer points on the SAT.[55] In other words, a white student whose family earns $200,000 in annual income could be expected to score more than 250 points more than a white student whose family earns only $30,000, thanks to greater resources and prior class advantages. As a result of the class-bound nature of the SAT, two-thirds of all test takers who score 1300 or above (on the old 1600-point scale) are from the wealthiest twenty-five percent of all families, while only seven percent are from the lowest-income quartile.[56]

That SAT scores have little to do with one's ability is borne out by a number of studies and even data provided by the test makers, which indicate that at most perhaps twenty-two percent of the difference between students in terms of freshman grades can be predicted or explained by results on the SAT.[57] On average, the correlation is even lower, predicting as little as 17.6 percent of student grade differences in the first year of college,[58] and at elite schools, like the University of Pennsylvania (where a study on this issue was conducted), as little as 4 percent of the grade variation can be explained or predicted by SAT score differences.[59]

Further, the correlation between SAT scores and overall four-year college grades or graduation rates has been so low that it is essentially nonexistent, explaining no more than three percent of the difference between any two students, as even the makers of the test admit.[60] As for overall grades, a study of eleven selective colleges found that having an additional one hundred points on the SAT relative to another student was only correlated, at best, with one-tenth of a grade point higher GPA throughout college.[61] As for graduation rates and likelihoods, at the University of California, Berkeley (where affirmative action was eliminated and where conservatives argue less-qualified blacks and Latino/as were being admitted over more-qualified whites and Asians), evidence conclusively shows that SAT score differences between students explain "almost none of the variation in graduation rates."[62]

In any event, the correlation between test scores and freshmen grades is lower than the correlation between high school grades and college grades.[63] In fact, when a college considers an applicant's SAT score in making its admissions decision, by adding standardized test scores to a consideration of grades, the college only increases the chance of getting a better-qualified college student (in terms of future performance) by less than one percent, hardly a significant improvement, and hardly an indication that blacks are "unqualified" for the college slots they receive.[64]

Hard evidence of the irrelevance of SAT scores to college performance and ability has emerged from the University of Texas, which in 1996 was forced to eliminate its affirmative action program. In response to the court-ordered ban, Texas lawmakers who were concerned about the possible effect the new policy might have on students of color adopted what is now known as the "ten percent plan." This plan guarantees admission to the University of Texas system for all students graduating in the top tenth of their high school class, irrespective of SAT score. Lawmakers who created the new plan reasoned that students in low-income, mostly black, and Latino/a schools who work hard and place in the top ten percent of their schools should not be punished because of their lower test scores—themselves largely a function of the lower-quality instruction received in an unequal system.

Naturally, critics of affirmative action argued that the plan would result in the admission of less-qualified students. Their position was that a student who ranked only in the top third of an elite private school (but who would now be admitted only after all the "ten-percenters" had been accommodated, assuming there was still space available) might be a better student than someone in the top ten percent of an inner city school with less-demanding coursework. By not prioritizing SATs, they argued, standards would drop and the quality of the incoming classes at the University of Texas would decline. But, in fact, after two full years of the Texas program, those admitted under the ten-percent plan were actually outperforming their traditionally admitted counterparts.[65] Average first-year GPAs have risen and students coming from the top ten percent of their high schools have, on average, outperformed non-top-ten students, even when those non-top-ten students had SATs that were two hundred to three hundred points higher than those in the top decile.[66]

The other common standardized test taken by high school students and used by colleges to help make admission decisions is the ACT, which is no better than the SAT at predicting academic performance or ability. According to one study of students at Chicago State University, the ACT explained less than four percent of student differences in cumulative GPA throughout college, and although the graduating class of 1992 there had the highest average ACT score of any class at the school during the time of the study, it also registered the poorest academic performance of any class under consideration by the research.[67]

As for students of color, the ACT is particularly bad at predicting their college performance. One study, for example, found that while results on the ACT could explain twenty-eight percent of the grade differences between any two white students in their first year of college (even then, not as much as high school grades could explain), the test explained less than *seven percent* of the grade gaps between black students.[68] Roughly seventy-five percent of any given black student's freshman grades in college are completely unrelated to (and unpredicted by) ACT scores.

It is also worth noting that when students of color do score lower on certain standardized tests, this likely reflects parental economic status more so than actual ability, and that those students of color will often have overcome substantial hardship to attain a decent score, even though it may be somewhat lower than the scores of more-privileged students. Evidence from California is particularly instructive here, where black and Latino/a students admitted to the University of California with lower scores tended to have overcome greater obstacles than their white counterparts and were thus especially qualified for a University of California education, as made clear by the generally lower economic status of the families from which they came. The year before the affirmative action ban went into effect in the University of California system, eighty-three percent of white applicants had fathers with at least a college degree, whereas only 36.2 percent of black applicants and twenty-five percent of Latino/a applicants did. Additionally, the average parental income of white applicants (and Asians it should be noted) was roughly double that of black or Latino/a applicants.[69]

As a general rule, black students who attend selective colleges where affirmative action comes into play are far more likely than their white counterparts to have overcome family economic obstacles to achieve, including a greater percentage of single-parent homes with less income and wealth, and far less average parental educational background.[70] In fact, more than a third of black students at America's most selective colleges and universities come from highly racially segregated communities where they were regularly exposed to various forms of social disorder and neighborhood violence.[71]

When one considers the greater economic disadvantage at which such students find themselves, their school achievements were certainly as impressive as those of more affluent whites, even if their test scores were somewhat lower. Receiving a 1050, 1150, or 1200 on the SAT, despite coming from a lower-income family with less educational history, and attending schools with fewer resources and less-demanding class offerings is more impressive, after all, than receiving a 1300 or 1400 having attended better schools and coming from a family with more educational background that could pay for prep classes, tutors, and enrichment experiences. Because blacks are only six percent of students at the most affluent high schools in the nation, and whites are eighty-four percent of students at these schools, it is hardly untoward to consider the relative positions from which students came in order to attain a grade or score at a certain level.[72]

As if undergraduate tests were not flawed enough, tests given for admission to various types of advanced degree programs are equally inadequate for determining actual abilities. For example, when black and white seniors from the same elite universities and with equal grades in the same academic departments are compared, the black students tend to score far lower on the LSAT, indicating that test results hardly measure academic ability.[73] At many schools, the LSAT is even worse than the SAT at predicting performance. Despite having generally lower LSAT scores going into law school at Berkeley's Boalt Hall, black graduates in many years have done *better* than white grads on the state bar exam.[74] Studies estimate that scores on the LSAT can predict only about seventeen percent of the difference, at best, between two students in their first year of law school, and often has no predictive validity whatsoever.[75] What is more, the test fails to predict graduation rates and scores bear no relationship to future performance as an attorney.[76]

Among the reasons for the low predictive validity of the LSAT is the rather large standard error built into the test. According to the LSAC, the standard error of measurement is 2.6 points in either direction for any given test taker. In other words, a 156 on the LSAT (on a scale from 120 to 180) is likely to indicate proficiency between 153.4 and 158.6. Once these numbers are rounded, the resulting score band (within which score differences are considered random) would be 153 to 159, or a band that was seven points wide in all. In other words, there is no way to predict with confidence that a student who scores 160 is any more likely to succeed than one who scores 154, or that a student who scores 150 is more likely to succeed than one who scores 144, for that matter. These gaps are often large enough to result in admission being denied to applicants at selective schools; yet according to the LSAC they are essentially meaningless. Even this seven-point random swing is only accurate at a sixty-eight percent confidence level, meaning that there is still a one-third chance that the real ability of a test taker at any given score lies beyond the seven-point range.

To boost the test's confidence level to a more statistically rigorous (and thus accurate) ninety-five percent, and thereby more or less ensure that a test taker's likely abilities were truly being gauged, the standard error of measurement, which is normally 2.6 points in either direction, would have to be doubled to 5.2 points in either direction. The result of such a reconfiguration is that the random score band would expand from a seven-point range to an eleven-point spread.[77] In other words, the more accurate the prediction of the LSAT, the larger the random error becomes, such that there is virtually no way to predict that one student is going to perform better in law school than another, unless that first student scores twelve or more points higher than the second student on the LSAT. It should be noted, as well, that the median LSAT score for white test takers is only ten points higher than the median for blacks—in other words, within the standard error for a ninety-five percent confidence prediction.[78]

In racial terms, use of the LSAT for admissions decisions operates as a virtual "tax" on aspiring minority law students, in that it screens out otherwise qualified applicants, whose grades are just as good as their white counterparts but whose test scores are lower (for reasons to be examined below). According to a comprehensive analysis of thousands of applicants to more than 175 law schools from 1994 to 1998, blacks and Latino/as have a far lower chance of admission than whites with equivalent grades, due to overreliance on the LSAT. According to the study, eighty-five percent of whites with college GPAs of 3.5 to 3.74 were admitted to law schools, compared to only seventy-six percent of African Americans and eighty percent of Latino/as. Among applicants with GPAs between 2.25 and 2.49, nearly half of whites were accepted, compared to only twenty-eight percent of blacks. Overall, seventy-two percent of white applicants to law school were accepted during the period 1994 to 1998, compared to sixty-nine percent for Asians, sixty-two percent for native Americans, sixty percent for Latino/as, and forty-six percent for blacks.[79] Not only do such figures prove the negative impact of test score considerations on qualified applicants of color, they also demonstrate the absurdity of reverse discrimination claims: plainly, whites are far more likely to be accepted to law school than their counterparts of color.

Studies on the GRE show that its ability to predict future performance is equally pathetic. Data from one thousand graduate departments around the country, collected by the test makers themselves, indicate that the GRE can only predict or explain, at best, nine percent of the variation between two students in their first year of grad school.[80] Additional studies by independent sources have placed the explanatory and predictive value of the GRE at no more than six percent in terms of first-year graduate school grade differences between two students. These correlations are so low that researchers have called the test "virtually useless."[81] Specifically, the GRE appears to underpredict the academic abilities of black students. As one study in particular discovered, black graduate students at the University of Florida with low GRE scores actually outperformed white students with high GRE scores, in terms of their grades in graduate school.[82]

Analysis of test score relevance for long-term professional success and accomplishment reveals that, here, the correlations are even lower. Studies on the relationship between GRE scores and the workplace performance of scientists, business executives, and other professionals have found the relationship to be virtually nonexistent and sometimes even *negative*. In other words, the higher students' GRE score the *less* their future professional success.[83] Likewise, a study of graduates from the University of Michigan Law School found that students who were admitted with high LSAT scores typically demonstrated lower levels of community leadership and community service after graduation and had no greater future income levels than those with average or lower scores.[84]

As for medical school, entrance exams are no better at that level for selecting the most qualified students. MCATs predict no more than sixteen percent of the difference between students, and even then only in science classes during the first two years of study. As students move to the clinical rotation stage, however, their MCAT scores prior to admission have no noticeable effect on (or relationship to) their success or failure, or the quality of their performance.[85] According to the *Journal of the American Medical Association*, students admitted to the University of California, Davis, School of Medicine with the help of affirmative action had academic and work records *after* admission that were equal to their white classmates.[86] Furthermore, a study by the Association of American Medical Colleges found that blacks who had successfully finished their first two years of medical school had generally scored lower on their entrance exams than whites who by that time had flunked out.[87]

Graduation and Grade Gaps Do Not Reflect Ability Differences: Debunking Mismatch Theory

Despite the evidence above, the right insists that standardized tests are valid indicators of actual academic ability, and for proof of this claim, they turn to what they consider the ultimate validating fact: namely, that students of color graduate from colleges at far lower rates than their white counterparts, and generally receive lower grades during their time as students. To conservatives, this indicates that once admitted with the help of "preferences," these students were in over their heads and thus underperformed in class, or were unable to finish their schooling at the school to which they were admitted. For critics of affirmative action, this is more than enough reason to eliminate so-called preferences for students of color. In fact, they argue, eliminating such programs would be doing black students a favor, since, after all, their interests are not served by being cast into academic waters they are not prepared to navigate.[88] In other words, as writers like Thomas Sowell explain, there is a "mismatch" between their actual skills and the schools into which they are admitted. Perhaps if they attended less prestigious schools they would do fine, but throwing them in over their heads is doing them no favors at all.[89] In truth, there are multiple problems with this line of argumentation.

First, to claim that grades and racial graduation gaps justify cutting back on student of color admissions, since presumably these gaps prove they are less capable of success than their white counterparts, sets up a particularly interesting corollary; one that few critics of affirmative action would be willing to acknowledge, of course. Namely, by this logic, schools would also be justified in admitting fewer male applicants and boosting the number of admits who are women; after all, female students consistently have higher GPAs and graduate at a higher rate than their male counterparts, even when their SAT scores are identical.[90] Needless to say, no critic of race-based affirmative action who argues that racial graduation gaps prove lesser black merit also argues that gender gaps in graduation rates prove lesser male merit.

As for graduation rates, differences between blacks and whites are often not that large, and even when they are there is little reason to assume this indicates the students of color are truly less capable. For example, blacks at elite schools like Yale, Harvard, and Princeton graduate at rates above ninety percent, hardly different from the white graduation rates at these schools.[91] At the University of Virginia, despite average SAT scores that are almost 250 points lower than the average for whites, black students graduate at a rate of eighty-four percent, hardly different than the white rate of ninety-three percent.[92] In fact, in virtually all cases, the more selective the college, the lower the rate of black dropouts, despite that such students tend to have much lower SAT scores than their white counterparts.[93] At the most selective schools, black graduation rates tend to be nearly twice as high as black graduation rates in general,[94] meaning that far from throwing black students in over their heads, these schools appear to be challenging their black students to outperform their counterparts at less selective institutions.

According to longitudinal data going back twenty years, black students in elite schools are, on average, between four and five percent more likely to graduate than blacks at less selective schools, at any given test score level.[95]

It is especially interesting to hear critics of affirmative action argue that blacks would be better off going to less selective schools where ostensibly their skill level would match up better with the quality of the instruction offered. After all, if blacks graduate at *lower* levels at these less selective schools, what these voices are essentially arguing is that blacks would be better off attending a school where their odds of graduating were *lower*, than attending a school where their odds of graduating were higher, simply because the gaps between their graduation rates and those of whites were larger in the latter group. It is hard to imagine that many black students would feel that way. It is, after all, small solace to a student who did not graduate from the less elite school that lots of whites also did not graduate.

Ultimately, although it is true that the general rate at which blacks graduate is well below the rate for whites, there is no reason to assume that this gap is caused by the lower qualifications of black students. For example, as Claude Steele has noted, when he closely examined the performance of white and black students at one particularly selective university, he found that even those blacks with combined SATs of 1400-plus (out of 1600) had dropout rates that were more than three times the rates for comparable whites. In fact, as many as a third of these high-scoring black students failed to graduate from their chosen institution.[96]

Likewise, the graduation rate gaps between whites and blacks, as well as gaps in college GPA, remain large even for students with the *exact same* SAT scores,[97] and the gap between SAT score and performance is highest for blacks at the *upper level* of test performance. In other words, blacks who score the *highest* are the most likely to underperform, relative to their white counterparts.[98] In fact, black students with only a C+ average at the above-mentioned college studied by Claude Steele, of the Stanford Psychology Department, had standardized test scores that averaged in the ninety-eighth percentile, while whites with those grades typically had scored only in the thirty-fourth percentile on the same standardized tests.[99] Ultimately, this means that even better-prepared black students will often underperform their white counterparts academically. Since the right presumes these test scores indicate ability, if blacks who score higher do worse in college than whites who score lower, how could lesser merit truly explain these racial gaps in grades and graduation rates? If anything, the fact that blacks at a particular SAT/ACT score do worse in college than whites at that same score (or lower) only proves that the tests say very little about ability per se, and likewise that GPA does not necessarily correlate with levels of preparation or ability either, as measured by these tests. In other words, it is clearly not for lack of academic merit that blacks underperform their white counterparts. Rather, financial obstacles, hostile racial climates on many campuses, and other non-merit factors influence and affect the success of black students in colleges and universities.

Indeed, financial concerns alone can explain a significant portion of the difference in completion rates. Black students are more likely to come from lower-income families, and in fact, at selective colleges and universities (which are typically among the most expensive in the country as well), the average black student comes from a family with half the median income of the average white student and one-third the income of the typical Asian student's family.[100] One-fourth of blacks at selective colleges live in families that rent their homes or apartments, compared to only six percent of white student's families, and whereas one out of six black students at selective colleges has spent some portion of their lives on welfare, only one in twenty-five white students has spent time on public assistance.[101]

This disparity in economic background has significant ramifications for the likelihood of students completing college, since the net costs for college for low-income students remains between $5,000 and $6,000 even after financial aid,[102] and since black students' families are only one-third as likely as white families to be able to pay the entire cost of their child's education.[103] On average, black students' families are only able to cover about forty-two percent of the cost of college at the nation's most selective schools, while white families are able to cover, on average, roughly seventy-four percent of the total cost.[104] Studies have found that students from low-income families (who are disproportionately persons of color) are less likely to graduate from college than more affluent students, even when they are identically prepared in terms of having taken a vigorous high school curriculum and scoring highly on standardized tests, with lower-income students at this level graduating at a rate of only sixty-two percent compared to eighty-five percent for similarly "qualified" affluent students.[105] Indeed, once total socioeconomic status—including wealth and asset levels—is held constant and only similarly situated white and black students compared, there is no racial difference in graduation rates.[106]

That the higher black dropout rate in mostly white schools is more about campus climate and feelings of isolation than ability is borne out by evidence that blacks in historically black colleges and universities (HBCUs) have graduation and accomplishment levels comparable to whites in mostly white schools,[107] and graduate at rates that are significantly higher in HBCUs than in historically white colleges and universities.[108] Indeed, although only sixteen percent of African Americans attend HBCUs, these institutions turn out nearly thirty percent of all black college graduates, graduates who are clearly highly competent students, and indeed go on to receive three-quarters of all graduate degrees awarded to blacks in the United States.[109]

Such results are likely due to the validating experiences and feelings of belonging, which are often more plentiful in such settings. Research has confirmed that feelings of attachment to an institution are extremely important in predicting whether or not black students will graduate from an institution of higher learning, and that such feelings are far harder to come by at mostly white schools, because of the climate to which so many students of color are subjected, overtly or subtly.[110]

Likewise, that blacks at schools of roughly equal selectivity often graduate at wildly different rates suggests that at those historically white institutions where blacks do quite well, something about the campus climate and support services available to students of color is assisting their success, despite lower test scores on average. Thus, while the graduation rate for blacks at the University of California, Berkeley, is only sixty percent, not far away in Palo Alto, at Stanford—a private school of the same general selectivity as Berkeley—the black graduation rate is eighty percent, twenty percentage points higher, meaning that blacks at Stanford are an entire one-third more likely than their Berkeley counterparts to graduate. And, indeed, Stanford does provide a more extensive array of support services for all students than does Berkeley, in large part because of its wealth and ability to do so, and the fact that as a smaller school, Stanford can concentrate services on each student more efficiently.[111] The result is that black students at Stanford, with lower scores than whites, still graduate at a high level, while blacks at Berkeley with comparable scores will be far more likely not to finish their education at the University of California. In neither case are SAT scores dispositive of student ability; rather, a series of often intangible issues relating to school climate will affect graduation rates for all students, but especially those in the extreme minority.

For final confirmation of the irrelevance of SAT score to student ability or college performance as reflected in graduation rates, consider the findings of a recent study by the Century

Foundation, which examined the differences in graduation rates based on SAT scores. Although supporters of standardized testing have long claimed that students with higher SAT scores have the best chance of graduating and, thus, affirmative action results in the selection of less capable—and ultimately less likely to succeed—students, the evidence casts a fatal blow to such a notion.

Results from hundreds of highly selective colleges around the nation make it clear that as long as a student admitted to the schools in question scores at least 1000 (out of 1600) on the SAT—well below the average for most elite colleges' freshmen classes—they are roughly as likely to graduate as their higher-scoring counterparts. Indeed, the graduation rate for students at elite colleges whose score was between 1000 and 1099 is eighty-six percent, compared to eighty-five percent for those who score between 1100 and 1199, and not much different statistically speaking from the graduation rates for those with scores of 1300 or better, at ninety-six percent. Furthermore, students at elite schools with SAT scores of 1200 have the same likelihood of graduating as students with scores above 1300.[112]

Interestingly, even students who score between 900 and 999 graduate from elite colleges at a rate of sixty-one percent, which is certainly lower than higher-scoring students, but not at a level that would indicate that they are unqualified to attend such schools.[113] Further, this rate is the same rate at which such students graduate from the least-selective schools, indicating that what determines a student's likelihood to graduate is not SAT score relative to the "difficulty" of the institution, but other factors such as financial burdens or campus climate. Since lower-scoring students will disproportionately be from lower-income families, the factor that is likely causal with regard to their failure to matriculate is their family's economic status, not their inability to succeed.

A few other points also stand out from the Century Foundation report: namely, students with scores between 1000 and

1099 are more likely than students scoring 100 to 199 points higher to graduate from colleges in the three most selective tiers, and students with 1300 or better on the SAT are *less* likely to graduate from the least selective schools than students scoring only 1100. So, if likelihood of graduating is to be the standard for determining who should and should not be admitted to a certain school, this would mean that the least selective schools should actually reject the top students in terms of test scores—despite their superior abilities—and instead choose students who are significantly less qualified (to the extent we believe test scores indicate real qualifications).[114]

In fact, to base admissions decisions on the odds of students graduating as evidenced by test scores would lead to some particularly bizarre results. For example, although students with 1300 or better on the SAT do indeed have the highest rates of graduation from first- and second-tier schools, and although students with scores between 1200 and 1299 rank second in terms of graduation rates, below 1200 things are considerably more complicated. In the most selective schools, students with scores between 1000 and 1099 actually graduate at a slightly higher rate than students who score 1100 to 1199, so by conservative logic should be admitted ahead of their seemingly more "qualified" counterparts. Likewise, in the second-tier schools, not only do students scoring 1000 to 1099 graduate at higher rates than students scoring between 1100 and 1199, but so do those students who scored between 900 and 999. So by conservative logic, even these sub-1000 scorers should be admitted before students who scored as many as 299 points above them!

Indeed, top scorers on the SAT should be admitted first at all but the *least* selective schools, where they should only be let in after students scoring 199 to 499 points lower. Low scorers, on the other hand, should be admitted last at the top and bottom levels of selectivity, but in the middle tiers of selectivity, they should actually be chosen ahead of applicants who scored 199 to 299 points higher. As if these configurations were not bizarre enough, middle-range scorers (1100 to 1199) should be accepted first at the least selective schools, last in the medium-selectivity schools, and next to last in the top schools, after those applicants scoring as many as 199 points below them.[115]

Of course, even if the correlation of test scores to grades and graduation rates was a perfect 1.0 (which it is clearly not), this would not necessarily mean anything in terms of the legitimacy of the test at predicting black potential, nor would it necessarily justify using the SAT as a measure of ability when determining admissions to college. Consider a simple thought experiment to understand why this is so.

Imagine that we could construct a society where racism was blatant against blacks, enshrined in law and custom, and where everyone basically agreed that discrimination was an everyday occurrence, in education and other settings. Imagine, in other words, that we could resurrect the apartheid system that existed in the United States for dozens of generations. Now, in such a society we would expect black standardized test scores to be well below white scores, even if blacks and whites were equally capable, simply because they had been given inferior preparation and instruction within the school system. Likewise, we would expect that once black students got in to college they would do worse than whites, because in our imaginary (or once quite real) society, racism would be so pervasive that even those blacks who are quite capable would face discriminatory treatment after gaining admission to a given school. So, in this hyperracist society, the correlation between black test scores and grades in college would be very high, perhaps perfect, because blacks would not only bomb the test but also do poorly in class. But would this perfect or near perfect correlation actually tell us anything about black potential? Of course not. It would merely tell us that racism not only drives down test scores but also can affect grades. No surprise here. It surely would not justify keeping blacks out of any given school, but rather would justify eliminating the racism that produced both results.

Indeed, the real-world situation for blacks in college is more like that described in this hypothetical than most Americans might like to admit. Black college grades are, after all, lower than white college grades, much as their average test scores are lower. However, even when comparing only whites and blacks who had identical SAT scores and grades in high school, black college grades remain lower than those for whites: as much as a third of a letter grade lower.[116] In other words, even when black students are equally "qualified" under the criteria preferred by the right, they still underperform their white counterparts, meaning that there must be something about the college experience that results in this underperformance. Research suggests a large part of that explanation would involve racial hostility on campus, which can drive down black performance relative to ability.[117]

As with undergraduate performance, the likelihood of graduating from law school is also largely unrelated to performance on the LSAT. In a comprehensive examination of law school applications, admissions decisions, and test scores, Wightman found that the majority of students of color who would have been denied admission under straight test score/grade criteria (and thus likely excluded in the absence of affirmative action) would have been excluded despite their ability, as evidenced by the fact that they did indeed go on to graduate. Furthermore, between seventy-five and eighty-eight percent of those students of color who would have been blocked from admission under strict "merit" criteria go on to pass their respective bar exams, indicating once again their ability and qualifications to practice law, irrespective of initial admissions test scores.[118] When we consider the overall bar passage rates of persons admitted under affirmative action—including those who passed by their third try—the differences between these students and non-affirmative action admits are insignificant. Although affirmative action admits are less likely to pass on their first try, there is no evidence that graduates who pass the bar on their first attempt end up more effective or successful lawyers.

Indeed, if affirmative action were abandoned and law schools adopted straight "merit" criteria based on LSATs and grades, it is possible that as few as twenty-two percent of black law school applicants would receive admission to any law school, to say nothing of the more prestigious schools—this despite their proven ability once admitted currently, as well as their ultimate success as lawyers.[119] As a study of graduates from the University of Michigan Law School found, without affirmative action as much as eighty percent of all graduates of color from the school would have been denied admission; yet these graduates were no less successful than their non-affirmative action counterparts after finishing school.[120]

Finally, right-wing arguments about test scores predicting graduation rates beg an obvious yet usually unasked question: namely, is it really desirable or legitimate to base admissions decisions on the likelihood of a student graduating, and thus preferring those with the best odds of doing so? Although such a criterion might appear to make sense at first glance, the fact is that it would actually justify making admissions decisions purely on the basis of whether or not an applicant's parents received college degrees, for this is the most important single factor in determining if a student will or will not graduate.[121] Yet no one would argue that colleges or graduate-level institutions should make their admissions decisions this way, using what amounts to aristocratic criteria, because doing so would perpetuate preexisting advantages and disadvantages, across and within racial and economic groups.

As for grades, the right argues that blacks are obviously in over their heads at selective colleges since they generally receive lower grades than their white and Asian counterparts. But not only does this argument overlook the nonmerit reasons for lower black grades (such as hostile racial climates, financial concerns, etc.), but it also makes the false assumption that students who graduate at the bottom of a college class are ipso facto less capable. The assumption is false because it ignores the simple fact that in every graduating class someone will always graduate last, or in the bottom half, but nonetheless deserve (and receive) their degree.

We do not, after all, tell the bottom third of the class that they cannot graduate. And if affirmative action were abolished tomorrow, there would still be someone graduating last in the class. That person might be white, and perhaps the bottom third of the class would be whiter than before. But would that now mean that the whites in question were unqualified and should have been turned away at the time of admission? Of course not. It is like the old saying goes: What do you call someone who graduates last in his class at medical school? Doctor. Since every one hundred additional points on the SAT is only associated with, at most, a boost of five to six percentile points in terms of class rank (i.e., the difference between graduating at the thirtieth or thirty-fifth percentile), it hardly seems logical to base admissions decisions on the notion that SAT scores are indicative of academic ability or likely success.[122]

It should also be noted that alternative forms of student assessment, largely unrelated to so-called cognitive ability, but highly related to students' experiences with marginalization, actually do as good a job of predicting college grades as the SAT. One tool, known as the Noncognitive Questionnaire (NCQ), assesses applicants to college on the following criteria: positive self-concept; their understanding of racism and ability to deal with it; emphasis on long-term over short-term goals; availability of supportive persons or networks to which they could turn in a crisis; successful leadership experience, and demonstrated community service. These criteria, seemingly unrelated to future academic performance, actually are just as likely to predict college grades as more traditional tools like the SAT.[123] However, they, unlike standardized tests, tend to improve the odds of admission for students of color.

In other words, there are assessment tools that would boost access for students of color, even while maintaining high levels of academic quality at the nation's colleges and universities. That most schools opt for the traditional methods, even as they exclude people of color and bear no better relationship to performance than these other tools, speaks to the extent to which educators continue to downplay the importance of racial equity and, returning to the thesis developed in the earlier sections of this book, the extent to which whites continue to be favored in admissions to colleges.

Black and Latino/a Test Scores Reflect Effects of Racism, Not Merit

One reason that blacks score lower on the SAT is because they receive inferior preparation in high school. Blacks with achievement test scores comparable to whites are disproportionately placed in remedial classes, where they receive inadequate instruction to prepare for the SAT,[124] and blacks and Latino/as are far less likely to be placed in advanced classes, even when achievement test scores would justify such placement.[125] By virtue of being tracked away from academic classes, these students of color end up ill-prepared to take college admissions tests. Students in higher tracks receive more instruction and are asked to do anywhere from forty percent to three times more homework than students in lower-track classes.[126]

As mentioned previously, schools serving mostly black and Latino/a students only offer a third as many advanced courses as their mostly white counterpart institutions.[127] This "curricular apartheid," then, directly affects test performance, a fact made obvious when we consider that black students who take AP courses score roughly as well as their white counterparts on the

SAT, meaning that given truly equal opportunity to take such classes, racial test score gaps would largely evaporate.[128]

Evidence from California is especially pertinent here. Despite claims that black and Latino/a applicants to the University of California prior to Proposition 209 were less qualified because they typically had SAT scores below their white and Asian counterparts, their lower scores are more properly seen as the result of having had less high-level instruction in high school. As Cecilia Conrad has demonstrated, prior to 209 and the 1995 University of California regents affirmative action ban, white students in California were forty percent more likely than blacks to have taken college prep classes and almost twice as likely as Latino/a applicants to have done so. Asian Pacific Islanders— often benefiting from the stereotype that "Asians are all good at math, and make the best students"—were twice as likely as blacks to have taken a college prep curriculum and two-and-a-half times more likely to have done so than Latino/as.[129] That whites and Asians were more likely to have taken these classes was not, of course, merely the result of personal choice. Instead, it was largely the result of such classes being less available in schools serving mostly black or Latino/a students.

Indeed, it is unequal schooling and not inherent lack of ability that explains the test score gaps between blacks and whites. Studies for years have found that although there are academic achievement gaps between whites and blacks, even at the beginning of the educational process—owing to the socioeconomic disparities between the two groups—over time, once exposed to unequal treatment and resources, these achievement gaps begin to grow. As a result, by the sixth grade the typical black student is two grade levels behind the average white student.[130] But essentially to punish black students for the effect of their unequal schooling, relative to whites, by further restricting access to top colleges is to hold the wrong parties responsible for the impact of racism and inequality.

The Consequences of Racism on Performance: Understanding "Stereotype Threat"

Another critical factor explaining lower black standardized test scores and academic performance is what psychologist Claude Steele and his colleagues have termed "stereotype threat." Black students are well aware of the negative stereotypes held about them by members of the larger society, and indeed report knowing of the negative ways in which they are viewed as early as age four, and usually before the age of nine.[131] As such, when blacks who are highly motivated and value education as a life goal take a standardized test and expect the results to be used to indicate cognitive ability, the fear of "living down" to the stereotype negatively affects their performance. Steele explains:

> In situations where one cares very much about one's performance or related outcomes—as in the case of serious students taking the SAT—this threat of being negatively stereotyped can be upsetting and distracting.... When this threat occurs in the midst of taking a high stakes standardized test, it directly interferes with performance ... for Black students, unlike White students, the experience of difficulty on the test makes the negative stereotype about their group relevant as an interpretation of their performance.... Thus they know as they meet frustration that they are especially likely to be seen through the lens of the stereotype as having limited ability.... This is an extra intimidation not experienced by groups not stereotyped in this way.[132]

Testing expert David White has observed stereotype threat with black test takers during practice tests given in a classroom setting, and notes:

> Some students will reject a correct answer as "too obvious," only to learn that it was the answer to a relatively easy item.

> This behavior can be a combination of self-doubt and test-taking strategy employed on a test that is touted as very hard. In contrast, a student who belongs to a group that is not stigmatized as less intelligent, and who performs with confidence ... will quickly pick the right answer without doubt or guile.[133]

To determine the cause of racial gaps on standardized tests, Steele and his colleagues devised a series of ingenious experiments. These involved taking two sets of equally qualified, then randomly divided black and white students and giving both sets questions from a GRE.[134] Psychology professor Shana Levin explains how the experiment played out:

> Participants were told either that the test was diagnostic of their intellectual ability—a situation high in threat because the stereotype about blacks' intellectual ability was made relevant to their performance on the test—or that the test was nondiagnostic of their intellectual ability—a situation low in threat because the negative stereotype was not related in any way to their performance on the test.... The results showed strong evidence of stereotype threat: blacks performed equal to whites in the nondiagnostic condition but performed more poorly than whites did in the diagnostic condition.[135]

Because real test-taking environments are high stress, and perceived as clearly high stakes, it is no surprise then that stigmatized group members might experience greater levels of stress on the exam, thereby increasing the likelihood of mediocre performance relative to their nonstigmatized counterparts. After all, those who can take the test without fear of living down to a socially common stereotype if they happen to do poorly would have one less thing to concern them as they went about the business of trying to perform well, or even to prepare for the test beforehand.

Even academic performance in regular class settings can be affected by the fear of confirming negative stereotypes. After all, if black students fear confirming negative beliefs about their group in the eyes of teachers or other students, they would be likely to underperform in class as well, relative to groups who did not face the stigma of such stereotypes. As Steele explains:

> Like anyone, blacks risk devaluation for a particular incompetence, such as a failed test or a flubbed pronunciation. But they further risk that such performances will confirm the broader, racial inferiority they are suspected of. Thus, from the first grade through graduate school, blacks have the extra fear that in the eyes of those around them their full humanity could fall with a poor answer or a mistaken stroke of the pen.[136]

According to longitudinal data on students at the nation's most-selective colleges, the black students who are most likely to underperform relative to whites, in terms of grades in college, failing a class, or failing to graduate, are those blacks who are especially concerned about teacher perceptions of their ability and most vulnerable to stereotype threat. Indeed, according to the available evidence, much of the difference in black and white grades in the freshman year of college can be explained by the effect of stereotype threat and its resultant impact on black performance—significantly more in fact than is explained by different levels of previous academic preparation and financial background combined.[137] Likewise, students who meet various conditions that make them particularly vulnerable to stereotype threat are eight times more likely to fail a class in their first year of college than those who are at low risk.[138]

What this means in concrete terms is that, once again, black performance in college cannot be attributed to inadequate preparation or lack of ability, let alone cultural "dis-identification" with education as a value. Rather, black student performance, on tests and in class, is shaped by the effects of external stigma and racism. The awareness that their performance may well be filtered through the lens of others' biases lowers black performance relative to ability, and must be considered in evaluating the propriety of affirmative action. As Levin puts it, "The implications of this line of research are that tests, as measures of performance, are not only indicative of individual ability but also of institutional climate."[139]

Further confirmation of the importance of stigma and stereotype threat to black student performance comes from programs that have successfully *boosted* black achievement by directly challenging the conditions that might otherwise reinforce the stigma. For example, beginning in the mid-1970s, Berkeley Calculus Professor Philip Uri Treisman designed a mathematics workshop for freshmen, in large part to boost the performance of black students, who he noticed tended to do far worse than their white and Asian counterparts. Treisman noticed that the black students, more so than others, tended to study alone, while whites and Asians, especially the latter, tended to study in groups. Believing that the individualistic methods employed by black students were hurting their preparation, his workshops emphasized group techniques, intended to allow each student to participate in learning the material, but to reduce the burden on each individual student to "know everything." Although Treisman did not use the language of stereotype threat, the concept was very much in tune with the later research on that subject. After all, if black students fear confirming negative beliefs about their group, and tend to study on their own, they increase their personal burden for getting test questions right or wrong, and might thereby increase their own levels of stress.

By encouraging group study and by stressing that the workshop was not remediation for skill deficits, but rather to be seen as an honors "challenge" for students with significant untapped potential, Treisman directly challenged the self-doubt that might otherwise hold down black performance due to stereotype threat. Even though many of the students in his workshops had scored less than 400 (out of 800) on their math SAT, the results were astounding. At the end of the workshops, black participants were outperforming their white and Asian peers in class. What is more, black participants in the workshops went on to graduate from the university at rates that were identical to the overall average.[140]

On the other hand, more traditional approaches to closing the black–white test gap (such as boosting black preparation or raising black student expectations and positive attitudes about their abilities) are unlikely to succeed, according to the research on stereotype threat, because such methods fail to address the issue of external pressures not to confirm negative beliefs about one's group.[141] Indeed, strategies to encourage black students to study harder and become more prepared may only deepen the effect of stereotype threat, by raising the perceived stakes to the test taker, and reminding him or her in no uncertain terms of the way in which blacks are viewed by the dominant culture.

Bottom line: To the extent black college students underperform their white and Asian counterparts, this sad fact has little if anything to do with different levels of actual ability or even preparation. Rather, the achievement gaps are related to the persistent devaluation of blacks in the larger society, which renders black students particularly vulnerable to stereotype threat and the fear of confirming (if they do badly) the preexisting stigmatizing biases of the larger community. As such, to eliminate affirmative action because it ostensibly benefits less-qualified students of color and puts them in college slots for which they are unprepared is to ignore the nonmerit-based reasons for different performance levels, and it would be to compound further the initial injustices that have given rise to those racial performance gaps in the first place.

Racial Test Score Gaps as a Function of Test Design

Perhaps most telling, racial gaps on standardized tests are ultimately a function of the way that tests like the SAT are developed. Indeed, the gaps are all but built-in. As anyone who has taken the SAT or a similar test remembers, there is an experimental section on the exam—either an extra verbal or extra math section—which contains questions that are not counted toward a student's score. The section exists as a way to "pretest" questions for potential use on future versions of the test. But as the testing company concedes, all questions chosen for future use must have produced (in the pretest phase) similar gaps between test takers as existed in the overall test taken at that time. In other words, a question is rarely if ever selected for future use if students who received lower scores overall answer that question correctly as often as (or more often than) those who scored higher overall. In practice, the racial implications of such a policy should be clear. Because blacks, Latino/as, and American Indian students tend to score lower on these exams than whites and Asians, any question in the pretest phase that black students answer correctly as often as (or more often than) whites would be virtually guaranteed *never to appear on an actual standardized exam.*[142]

In practice, questions answered correctly by blacks more than whites are routinely excluded from future use on the SAT. Although questions that whites answer correctly thirty percent more often than blacks are allowed to remain on the test, questions answered correctly even seven percent more often by blacks than whites have been thrown out.[143]

Although the rationale for this practice is not overtly racist—the testing company, for example, does not intentionally seek to maintain lower scores for blacks—the thinking has a racist impact. Essentially, the company's position is that for any question to have predictive validity (and what statisticians call biserial correlation), it should be answered correctly or incorrectly in rough proportion to the overall number of correct or incorrect answers given by test takers; but since the general scores have tended to exhibit a racial gap, such logic results in the virtual guarantee of maintaining that gap, as a function of test design.[144] The impact of such a policy is as ironic as it is harmful; after all, if certain verbal test questions were made less culturally biased, so that the racial gap shrunk or disappeared in the pretest phase, those questions would likely be thrown out, simply because—being less culturally biased—they failed to replicate the racial gaps produced by the full exam.

Interestingly, as testing expert Jay Rosner has demonstrated, the makers of the SAT could reduce the racial gap between whites and blacks while still maintaining the same level of overall test difficulty by simply choosing questions that, despite being of the same general level of complexity, exhibited less differentiation between white and black test takers. That, instead, they choose to perpetuate these differences by way of the questions they choose is not the result of following some inviolable principle of test validation, but rather is the result of their preexisting assumptions about how test takers should perform.[145]

For conservatives to show that affirmative action lowers the quality of students admitted to colleges, they would have to prove that tests like the SAT were valid indicators of ability and that students of color had been given an equal opportunity to prepare for these tests. But given the data on the inadequacy of these tests to predict performance, and the institutional inequity in schools that provides such unequal opportunity to prepare for the SAT, their ability to "prove" either of these claims is doubtful.

Some Preferences Are More Equal Than Others: White Racial Preference in Admissions

It is worth noting that for all the complaints about so-called preferences for students of color, affirmative action critics are remarkably silent about the much larger system of preferences that works to the benefit of the children of alumni. At most schools—and especially the elite colleges and universities with the most aggressive affirmative action programs—there are far more "legacy" admissions than there are students who benefit from affirmative action; and because of the historic barriers that for many generations excluded blacks and other students of color from those schools, almost all of the students admitted as legacies will be white and mostly affluent. At Ivy League schools, as just one example, ninety-six percent of living alums are white, meaning that almost all the beneficiaries of legacy preference will also be white.[146] In other words, there are far more middle-class, working-class, and poor whites being "bumped" from the college of their choice because of these handouts to legacies than are being bumped for all the students of color combined.

At Harvard, the admission rate for nonlegacies is fifteen percent, but for legacies the rate is nearly forty percent, despite that legacy applicants tend to have lower SAT scores than regular applicants. In fact, if the 1988 freshman class at Harvard had been admitted at the same rate as nonlegacies (in other words, had legacies not received "preferential treatment"), two hundred fewer legacies would have been admitted. This is a larger number than all the people of color admitted that year, with or without the help of affirmative action.[147] Nationally, anywhere from twelve to twenty-five percent of each freshman class at top schools will be filled by the children of alumni, which is far more than the number admitted because of so-called racial preference for people of color.[148]

Not only do conservatives rarely complain about, let alone seek to abolish, alumni preferences that benefit whites, but indeed many of the folks who complain about so-called preferences for people of color are quick to demand that such white preferences remain in place. In 1996, just one year after the regents of the University of California voted to abolish affirmative action in the University of California system, it was revealed that the same regents had been doling out slots at UCLA to the children of well-connected contributors and political allies.[149] Two years later, after public outcry, the regents voted to allow these special "backdoor" admissions for the well connected to remain in place, in addition to the preferences granted to children of alumni, who receive preferential review and can be admitted, despite lower GPAs.[150]

Along the same lines, the early admission programs operated by most elite colleges have a significant impact on freshman class compositions, far greater, in fact, than the impact of affirmative action efforts. These programs—which allow high school students to apply early on the understanding that if accepted they are committed to attending that particular school—exist because they make filling the freshman class quicker and cheaper for the colleges. Applicants in the early pool tend to be more affluent (which means they will need less financial assistance from the college), and their obvious desire to attend the school to which they apply early means that colleges have to worry less with wait lists or additional outreach efforts. Furthermore, since early admittees are going to attend the college to which they are accepted early, the percentage of accepted applicants who end up enrolling at that particular school will rise, much to the institution's benefits in elite rankings of "top colleges," which consider the "yield" rate (the percentage of students who are accepted who actually end up going to that school) to be a significant indicator of the school's desirability. Consideration as a "highly selective" and desirable school is additionally helpful to improving a college's bond rating, which in turn can save schools millions of dollars in interest paid to banks each year.

Because early admission generally requires that students have strong grades and test scores before beginning their senior year of high school, early admissions programs tend to favor those who come from schools with more resources in more affluent communities. This not only works against students of color but also tends to harm working-class and poor white college applicants. For students of color or lower-income whites, early applications are risky. If students are accepted and then locked into attending the school to which they apply, it becomes impossible for such applicants' families to weigh competing financial aid offers, which would be a concern to all but the most affluent families.

According to recent studies, early admissions programs are a huge form of preferential treatment for those who are ready to commit to a particular school, irrespective of their actual "merit." Admissions rates for early applicants are often three times higher than the rates for applicants in the regular applicant pool. One study of applications and admissions at fourteen selective colleges found that applying early was worth as much as one hundred points on the SAT and resulted in generally less "qualified" students being accepted.

So for the sake of simplicity and getting the most "committed" (and most able to pay) students, colleges are willing to sacrifice so-called "qualifications." Yet, this kind of preferential treatment, which results in squeezing out far more white college applicants than all the affirmative action programs put together, receives no mention by those who seek to exploit white racial resentment toward people of color.[151]

THE MYTH OF STIGMA

In an attempt to portray themselves as mightily concerned about the well-being of people of color, critics of affirmative action are increasingly turning to an argument that steers the discussion away from the image of reverse discrimination, "angry white men," or even "less qualified" black and brown applicants. This argument posits that persons who are able to benefit from affirmative action programs will be stigmatized by the knowledge of such preferences, whether or not they actually received a boost as a result. They may develop self-doubt, never sure that their successes in life were their own, and this self-doubt can be crippling not only to self-esteem but even to overall work effort. This is the position of many black conservatives, for example, most prominently among them, Shelby Steele and John McWhorter.[152] Such critics also point out what they consider the insulting irony of affirmative action: namely, that so-called racial preferences imply that blacks are less capable than others and need special dispensation to succeed. In other words, they claim, affirmative action is fundamentally racist because it views its beneficiaries as incapable of making it on their own.

But to claim that blacks are stigmatized and scandalized by affirmative action is to imply that such persons would have been better off without such efforts. Yet a simple glimpse at the rather obvious benefits of affirmative action for African Americans calls into question how reasonable it is to assume that the impact of such programs has been detrimental. For example, not only has affirmative action opened a wide array of professions to blacks that had been more or less off-limits previously, but it has also helped boost the share of black students going to college and graduate school, sometimes dramatically. In 1970, only 4.5 percent of blacks had a bachelor's degree, but by 1990 that number had grown to thirteen percent, and has only continued to grow since.[153] Surely, it is not logical to think that black self-esteem would have been better off in the absence of these improvements in life chances and opportunities; yet that is essentially what conservatives are saying.

Also, given ongoing black support for affirmative action, those who claim blacks are harmed by such policies are in effect arguing either that "black folks" are too unintelligent to realize what affirmative action is doing to them, or perhaps that blacks enjoy being stigmatized. How else, after all, could one interpret survey data from the Gallup Corporation, suggesting that only twelve percent of African Americans support reducing or eliminating affirmative action, while fifty-three percent actually want to *increase* affirmative action efforts, and most of the remaining third believe it should be left as is? Why would blacks seek to maintain or expand affirmative action, by more than a six-to-one margin over those seeking to scale it back or end it, if indeed affirmative action were bad for African American self-esteem? Are blacks just too stupid to see when they are being insulted, or do they simply not mind being insulted? To accept the stigma argument requires first believing that the answer to at least one of these fundamentally racist questions is yes.[155]

Additionally, for conservatives to criticize affirmative action for supposedly branding blacks as inferior and thereby stigmatizing them seems more than a little hypocritical given the way in which the right greeted a book like *The Bell Curve*, by Charles Murray and Richard Herrnstein. *The Bell Curve*, after all, did not imply that blacks were inferior to whites and Asians, it said so *blatantly*, by arguing that black IQ in the United States and African IQ are much lower than white and Asian IQ, and that this difference relates to real differences in cognitive ability, differences that are mostly genetic in origin. Additionally, Murray and Herrnstein argue that blacks are genetically predisposed, because of lower intelligence, to everything from crime, to bearing children out of wedlock, to getting speeding tickets.[155] Yet when the book was released in the fall of 1994, and soon became a best-seller, not only did conservatives not criticize it for stigmatizing blacks and arguing that they were inferior, but indeed *no* prominent conservative criticized it,[156] many (such as William F. Buckley's *National Review*) praised it in spite of the controversy it generated,[157] and Murray was invited to speak to the GOP congressional delegation, a few months after the Republicans took control of Congress in 1994.[158]

Further, Murray's work on *The Bell Curve* was underwritten by several grants from the Bradley Foundation, a conservative think tank in Milwaukee, which is well respected in mainstream conservative circles. Bradley, in fact, funds many of the organizations and individuals who claim affirmative action stigmatizes blacks, including black conservative Ward Connerly, who received Bradley money to write his book *Creating Equal.* Connerly's organization, the American Civil Rights Institute, has also received more than half-a-million dollars from Bradley in recent years.[159] So the very group that helped fund a book *saying* blacks are genetically inferior then funds conservative activists who argue affirmative action is bad because it *implies* blacks are inferior! Bradley is also one of the leading organizational forces behind the movement to establish vouchers in public schools, ostensibly to help low-income kids of color escape bad schools and attend better public or private ones (at least that is their public argument),[160] and yet it funded a book which argues that there is basically nothing that can be done for low income blacks because they are genetically damaged.

It is also worth pointing out that the persons who express this outpouring of concern for the psychological well-being of blacks, presumably damaged by affirmative action programs, say remarkably little about the stigma that must surely attach to the children of alumni who receive substantial preferences in college admissions, as we have seen. They also have no concern, apparently, for the self-image of children from wealthy families who inherit their parents' fortunes, or about the self-esteem of affirmative action critics like Ward Connerly, for that matter, who admits that his appointment to the Board of Regents at the University of California, from which perch he began his assault on so-called racial preferences, came about only because of his long-standing friendship with then-Governor Pete Wilson, and the fact that he had made more than $120,000 in contributions to Wilson's political campaigns.[161]

For that matter, why do they exhibit no concern for the whites who have *always* received racial preference, unrelated to actual ability? If affirmative action has somehow managed to cripple black self-image, imagine what self-doubt must surely characterize the white community, with its centuries-long racial preferences in jobs, education, immigration policy, housing, and criminal justice? Perhaps we should dispatch therapists to the American suburbs to provide counseling to those families who obtained homes under blatantly preferential FHA and VA loan programs, as discussed in the first chapter?

In the final analysis, to claim that affirmative action is the reason for occasional self-doubt on the part of blacks or other people of color completely ignores that racism *itself* causes that self-doubt, or can do so, with or without affirmative action. Racism *itself* assaults the dignity and self-esteem of its targets, by consistently blocking them from rising to the levels of their ability and ambitions. How can someone's self-esteem be more damaged by getting a job or college slot than by *not* getting one? How can one be more stigmatized, in effect, by being given a chance to prove oneself, than by not being given that chance?

Furthermore, once people of color get into a college or get a job, even with the help of affirmative action, they still have to perform in order to succeed—either to get a good grade or keep their job—and as such, whatever stigma could even theoretically attach initially to such a boost would surely dissipate once they had to demonstrate their abilities, and did so. Indeed, an analysis of more than two hundred studies, published in the *Journal of Economic Literature* (a publication of the American Economics Association) found that those who benefit from affirmative action perform equal to or better than their white male counterparts, even if their initial credentials were somewhat less impressive.[162] So, apparently, whatever "stigma" the beneficiaries of affirmative action are suffering is of negligible impact in terms of their performance, in which case one would have to assume said stigma would then be eliminated, as would any perceptions on the part of others that those who had reaped the benefits of affirmative action were somehow less qualified.

Finally, of course, there is no logic whatsoever to the notion that defenders of affirmative action perceive blacks to be inferior, or in need of special assistance because of some inability to succeed on their own. Quite the contrary, defenders of affirmative action are overwhelmingly of the opinion that people of color are every bit as capable as anyone else, but that racism and discrimination are real impediments to even the most qualified and most hardworking person of color. Racism and discrimination mean *something* and actually have an effect, and this effect says nothing about the talents of its victims, but rather about the tenacity of the systemic process by which such persons are often excluded from full opportunity.

The Myth of the Asian Model Minority

Among the more prominent arguments made by critics of affirmative action is that Asian Pacific Americans have proved that everyone can make it in America if they are willing to expend the effort. Since Asian income is actually higher than white income and since Asians do especially well in school, this proves racism is no longer a substantial obstacle to peoples of color, and that if blacks and Latino/as would merely respond to the opportunity structure as Asians have managed to do, they would accomplish just as much.[163] By casting Asian Pacific Americans as a "model minority," conservatives imply that the failures of blacks, especially, are the fault of blacks themselves. But the model minority concept is not only cynical and manipulative, as will be seen, it is also premised on false notions and terribly misinterpreted data.

To begin with, the history of the model minority imagery should give us pause regarding its ultimate legitimacy. Although the argument has gained special traction in recent years, the fact is the portrayal of Asians as model minorities has a long and dubious pedigree. The term "model minority" to describe Asians in the United States was first used in 1960, in *The New York Times Magazine*, in an article about the success of Japanese Americans, and how their superior family cultures prevented them from becoming a "problem minority." Later that year, *U.S. News & World Report* ran a similar piece, this time about Chinese Americans.[164] In both cases, and in subsequent pieces, journalists were quite obviously contrasting these "model minorities" to those seen as "problems," which meant, ultimately, African Americans. That such articles were being run at the height of the civil rights movement, at a time when the "problem" minorities were agitating for significant social change, should not be lost on anyone. It was as if the authors were saying that blacks should stop fussing about apartheid and just work harder, ultimately the same argument made today by those who hold up the Asian Pacific American community as evidence of what blacks need to do to succeed.

But beyond the ignoble origins of the model minority myth, the argument itself is thoroughly flawed, for a number of reasons.

First, the claim that Asians have "made it" in America ignores the preexisting advantages that most Asians in the United States had upon their arrival here, advantages that would place them well above most blacks and Latino/as in the class structure. For example, unlike the black community, which is a cross section of persons with a wide array of skills, the Asian Pacific American community, mostly composed of voluntary immigrants, is by definition a more self-selected and, therefore, more advantaged bunch. Voluntary migrants from nations that are not contiguous to their country of destination tend to be those with the skills, money, and background needed to leave their country of origin in the first place, and to then be successful in their adopted lands. Indeed, with Asian immigrants to the United States, research has made clear that these immigrants tend to come from an occupational and educational elite within their own countries.[165] As Asia scholar Ezra Vogel explains, they are by and large the "cream of their own societies."[166]

In large measure, this preexisting class advantage for Asians in the United States has been maintained by way of immigration policies that largely favored high-skilled immigrants with educations over those without. As the Federal Glass Ceiling Commission discovered in the mid-1990s, between two-thirds and three-quarters of highly educated Asian Pacific Americans already had college degrees or were working on their degrees at the time of their arrival in the United States.[167] Thanks to immigration policies favoring those with college educations, Asian Americans today are two-thirds more likely to have a college degree than whites and nearly three times more likely than blacks to have a degree.[168] As just one example of how these policies favored immigrants with preexisting class advantage, consider that from 1966 to 1977 more than eight in ten immigrants from India had advanced degrees and training in such areas as science, medicine, or as engineers.[169]

So to compare the well-being of Asian Pacific Americans with that of blacks, for example, is absurd on the face of it. Blacks were not self-selected as voluntary immigrants, and so naturally will represent a broader cross section of background and abilities, unlike Asians who will, by and large, be a select group, hardly representative of some superior Asian culture or cultures. After all, given the rampant poverty that plagues millions of Asians in their countries of origin, it makes little sense to argue that Asian cultures are somehow superior to those of African Americans. Indeed, ethnic Koreans in Japan, as well as the Burakumin there—persons descended from a lower-caste group, not unlike the Dalits (untouchables) in India—consistently underperform economically and educationally compared with dominant Japanese members of the society. They are both targets of discriminatory treatment, and although they are largely indistinguishable in cultural terms from other Koreans or Japanese, they are consistently found at the bottom of Japanese society, and perform far worse than others in Japan or Korea with whom they share genes and culture. Black Americans have been situated more like the Japanese *Burakamin* than the typical Asian immigrant to the United States, and if comparisons are made between these two groups, as opposed to two groups with very different relationships to the power structures of their respective societies, we see dramatic similarities—similarities that suggest the importance of caste status to overall achievement.[170]

Further complicating the conservative image of Asian Americans as model minorities is the rather out-of-context data used to make the case. For example, the right argues that Asian family and household income is higher, on average, than even that for whites.[171] Surely, this suggests, everyone can make it in America if they are willing to try hard enough. But these data, although accurate so far as it goes, are highly deceptive and misleading. To begin with, data showing Asian Pacific Americans doing better than whites are always either *family* income data or *household* income data, and either way, this makes a huge difference. Asian Pacific American households and family units, for example, tend to have more members (thus, slightly higher incomes have to stretch across more persons) and also more earners per family, meaning that it takes more people working in an Asian family to earn only slightly more than a white family.

Indeed, the average household size for an Asian American family is 3.3 persons, compared to only 2.5 persons per white household. Asian American families, furthermore, are more likely than white families to have two wage earners, and nearly twice as likely to have three wage earners as white families.[172] Asian American families are also thirty-six percent more likely to have three or more persons living in the home, and almost two-thirds more likely to have five or more family members in the home, while whites are two-thirds more likely to live alone.[173] In other words, Asian income is stretched far more thinly than white income. The key figure is *per capita* income, and there, white income remains higher than income for Asian Pacific Americans, as much as $2,000 more per person per year.[174]

In fact, this comparison understates the wage advantage enjoyed by whites relative to Asians, because the white totals, whether looked at in terms of per capita income, family income, or household income, include Latino/a families, almost all of which are considered racially "white" in Census and Labor Department data of this nature. That Latino/a income, on a per person basis, family basis, or household basis is well below that for non-Hispanic whites and more on a par with African Americans, including their averages in the white income totals, artificially limits the apparent white income average and thereby artificially closes the income gap between whites and Asians.[175]

Interestingly, if anything, Asian incomes should be much higher than white incomes on average, for two reasons: first, the greater percentage of Asian Americans with college degrees, and second, the geographic concentration of Asians in high-income (and high cost of living) locations within the United States. Given these factors, for Asian Pacific Americans barely to edge out white families in terms of median annual income, and still to lag behind whites in terms of per capita income, suggests not only that Asians have not conquered racism and "made it," but rather, that they continue to face substantial bias despite their qualifications.

Since Asian Pacific American males are fifty-nine percent more likely than comparable white men to have a college degree, and Asian Pacific American women are sixty-three percent more likely than white women to have a college degree, we should logically expect them to earn considerably more than whites, on a per person basis, but this is, as noted above, not what happens in the real world.[176]

Furthermore, of the 12.5 million Asian Pacific Americans in the United States, half live in the American West, which is typically a much higher wage, and higher cost of living part of the country, while only nineteen percent of whites live in this high-wage region. On the flipside, only nineteen percent of Asian Pacific Americans live in the American South (typically a low-wage region), compared to fully one-third of whites who live there.[177] The three states with the largest Asian populations and a disproportionate share of the overall Asian American population are California, New York, and Hawaii, which rank thirteenth, fourth, and sixteenth in terms of average personal income—all within the top third of states.[178] Whereas slightly more than three-quarters of all Asian Americans are clustered in the higher-income regions of the United States (the West and Northeast), only forty-one percent of whites are found in these areas, and only twenty-eight percent of blacks.[179] In fact, sixty-two percent of Asian Americans live in just five states,[180] and more than half reside in just five cities: Honolulu, San Francisco, Los Angeles, Chicago, and New York City, all of which have much higher than average household incomes, as well as costs of living.[181] So although Asian American incomes will be high in relative terms, given where Asian American families tend to live, this "extra" income will not tend to go very far, and indeed the average disposable income and living standards for Asian Americans will remain well below that of whites.

This point is made even clearer if we look at metropolitan wage averages. While the overall metropolitan average income (which itself is far higher than the national average) was approximately $30,000 in 1996, in New York City the average income was $45,000 and in San Francisco it was $40,000. Because Asian Americans are more likely than whites to live in metropolitan areas, and twice as likely as whites to live in core urban areas, their average earnings should be expected to be higher, but their living expenses will also be far higher, meaning that their overall standard of living will still fall well below that of whites.[182]

Perhaps even more importantly, claims of Asian "success" obscure the fact that Asian Americans continue to suffer far higher rates of poverty than whites. In 2001, for example, Asian Pacific Americans were about thirty percent more likely than whites to be poor, and Asian Pacific American married couples were twice as likely as their white counterparts to be poor.[183] Even worse, the poverty rate for Asian Pacific American children is fully *double* that of white children.[184] Indeed, this may be an understatement of the gap between white and Asian American poverty, since, once again, white poverty totals include most Latino/a families. Since Latino/a poverty rates are comparable to black poverty rates, and far higher than the rates for non-Hispanic whites, including them in the data, as the Census Bureau does, artificially inflates the rate of white poverty, thereby making the gap between white poverty and Asian American poverty appear far smaller than it likely is.

Furthermore, if we examine relative poverty rates in those areas where Asian Americans tend to be concentrated geographically, such as Los Angeles, San Francisco, and New York City, for example, we discover that the poverty rate for Asian Americans in those places is twice as high as the white rates. In other words, it may be true that Asian Pacific American incomes are generally higher than incomes for whites, but this is because Asian Pacific Americans tend to be in higher-income parts of the country. Yet compared to whites in the same areas, Asian Pacific Americans are not doing particularly well. The only reason the "average" Asian Pacific American income is higher than the "average" white income is because the former group is so heavily concentrated in high-wage regions, while the latter is spread more evenly across the country. The proper comparison—whites and Asian Americans in the *same places*—demonstrates a persistent advantage to being white, and persistent disadvantages for Asians.[185]

Conditions are especially unfavorable for Southeast Asians, and this is worth noting precisely because these groups—Lao, Hmong, Vietnamese, Cambodian, and Thai—tend to more closely resemble African Americans and Latino/as in terms of their background status. Unlike most Chinese, Japanese, Indian, or Korean immigrants, for example, these group's members were largely desperation refugees. As such, they would be less likely to bring with them the preexisting class advantages that were so common for others. In the early 1990s, half of all Southeast Asian immigrants and refugees in the United States were living in poverty, with annual incomes of less than $10,000 per year on average.[186] Even Southeast Asians with *college degrees* were likely to remain poor. For example, two-thirds of Lao American and Hmong American college graduates live below the poverty line, as do nearly half of Cambodian Americans and over a third of Vietnamese Americans with degrees.[187]

What these data suggest is that the tendency to view "Asian Americans" as a monolithic, successful, and undifferentiated mass, so as to contrast their performance with that of African Americans and Latino/as is a cynical and deceptive tactic, which obscures the vast gaps that separate Asian Pacific Islanders in terms of their well-being in this country. This is true in terms not only of wages, but also of representation in institutions of higher education. So, for example, Chinese, Japanese, Koreans, and Indians are twice as likely to be enrolled in college in the United States as Hmong, Lao, native Hawaiians, or Samoans.[188]

Indeed, Asian "success" rhetoric ignores not just ongoing Asian poverty, but also real and persistent discrimination against Asian Americans, relative to whites. Overall, Asian Americans with a college degree earn, on average, eleven percent less than comparable whites, and Asian Americans with only a high school diploma earn, on average, twenty-six percent less than their white counterparts.[189] When Asian American men have qualifications that are comparable to those of white men, they still receive fewer high-ranking positions than those same white men. For example, Asian American male engineers and scientists are twenty percent less likely than white men to move into management positions in their respective companies, despite no observable differences in ambition or desire for such jobs. Likewise, only sixty-five board seats in major public corporations in the United States are held by Asian Pacific Americans, and Asian Pacific Americans are less than one percent of corporate directors at any level.[190]

Of course, beyond the statistical manipulation by those who trumpet the model minority theme, there are a number of additional points to be made. First, if white conservatives truly believe that Asians are somehow culturally superior and make for better employees, not only when compared to blacks, but even when compared to whites, then why are these persons not clamoring for a massive increase in immigration from Asian nations? Why not call for a flooding of the borders, if indeed Asians are so smart and hardworking that we could all learn something from them? Why not call for white male CEOs to step down from their positions atop American corporations and allow the corporations to be run, immediately, by Japanese managers, since, after all, they are among the model minorities on whom we can count to do such an amazing job because of their cultural superiority?

Furthermore, it seems obvious that the same individuals trumpeting the model minority concept would be the first to object if Asian Americans really began to supplant their own white children from college slots at elite schools, even if they did so by way of higher test scores and other merit indicators. To demonstrate the point, consider a hypothetical case. Imagine that next year the top thirty-five hundred applicants to the University of California, Berkeley, in terms of grades and test scores, were Asians and Asian Americans. Since there are only thirty-five hundred slots in the freshman class, does anyone actually think that the regents of the University of California system would sit back and allow the first-year class at their flagship institution to become *entirely* Asian? Or for that matter, even eighty percent, or seventy percent? How would white Californians react to such a development, including those who currently praise hardworking Asian kids for their education excellence and scholarly achievements? How would white alumni react if these "model minority" members were suddenly bumping *their* children, and not black and brown kids? To ask the question is to answer it.

To argue—as critics of affirmative action do—that Asians have "made it, so why can't blacks?"—is to misunderstand the issue of moral and ethical responsibility to correct the harms of wrongful actions, past and present. The fact is, even if we accept the notion that groups harmed by racism can "make it" without assistance, targeted opportunity, or affirmative action, that would not deny (or speak to in the least) the fact that society has as obligation to compensate the victims of injustice and to make them as whole as possible in the event of injury. If my leg, after all, were to be blown off in an industrial accident, it would hardly matter that many people with one leg go on to succeed. The issue of compensatory justice would remain, irrespective of what gains can be made without programs to assist those injured.

Perhaps what is saddest about the use of model minority imagery by those opposed to affirmative action is the way such argumentation is fairly calculated to pit blacks and Asians against one another, thereby keeping them fighting, rather than working together to overcome the race and class barriers that continue to injure them both. Several years ago, pollster Lou Harris asked a representative of the ultraconservative Heritage Foundation whether the right feared that its position might ultimately unite women and minorities, to which he was told, "It will never happen. We know full well that as much as each minority may feel victimized by discrimination or the lack of equal opportunity, the minorities will be at each other's throats and will never stick together."[191]

For the sake of racial equity and social justice, we had best hope that the folks at the Heritage Foundation are wrong in their assessment.

THE MYTH OF BLACK CULTURAL DEFICIENCIES AND ANTI-INTELLECTUALISM

In keeping with the model minority argument—which holds that Asian cultural values emphasize education and hard work, thereby explaining Asian success in schools and the job market—critics of affirmative action then claim that too much of black America *deemphasizes* educational pursuits, and thereby sabotages their own ability to succeed.[192] Among the arguments they put forth is the claim that low SAT and other standardized test scores among blacks are the fault, not of test bias or other forms of systemic inequality, but rather of the family structures so prevalent in the black community. Specifically, they suggest that a disproportionate share of single-parent homes in the African American community—itself a form of cultural pathology—harms black academic achievement, and that to boost outcomes for blacks and close these achievement gaps, something will need to be done about black family structure.[193] The arguments blaming black cultural traits for educational underachievement have become so popular that they are often espoused even by those who are not particularly conservative in orientation, such as Bill Cosby and Harvard Professor of African American Studies Henry Louis Gates.[194] But despite the commonality of these positions, they remain inaccurate and rooted in racist stereotypes.

Score gaps on the SAT between whites and blacks, for example, cannot possibly be related to cultural flaws, as if a mere vestige of "underclass" pathology, as demonstrated conclusively by the disturbing fact that black test takers from families with $70,000 or more in annual income score *lower* on the SAT, on average, than white test takers from families with less than $20,000 in annual income. Even worse, blacks from families with $50,000 in annual income, score lower, on average, than whites from families with less than $6,000 in annual income.[195] Even upper-income black students, then, are doing badly on exams like the SAT, despite coming from families that are overwhelmingly professional, educated, intact, and surely not "underclass." Such a fact points to reasons for their failure other than culture, and other than the *Bell Curve*–type biological argument, since successful black families would tend to be neither culturally nor biologically defective relative to the mainstream. If they were, after all, they would not have been very likely to become successful in the first place. In fact, such a phenomenon lends even more credence to the previously discussed culprit of "stereotype threat," since children from successful families would be the most likely to worry about the way they were perceived by others, relative to the common stereotypes of African Americans, and as such, might underperform relative to their actual ability levels.

Further demonstrating that "underclass" values or family structures can hardly explain racial test score gaps, consider that the kinds of students criticized as not valuing education sufficiently and the students of color who bomb the SAT are, almost by definition, two entirely different sets of people. Only forty-five percent of high school graduates even take the SAT, and in many states those are only those students who plan on going to elite schools.[196] Needless to say, "underclass" kids from impoverished homes (and certainly those who do not "value" education) are not likely to be taking a test to improve their chances of getting into Harvard.

Likewise, and contrary to the claims of some on the right, test score gaps beginning in elementary school cannot be explained by virtue of the greater percentage of single-parent homes in the black community.[197] When other factors, including family socioeconomic status, parental education, and the test scores of one's mother are held constant, there is simply no racial difference between five- and six-year-old cognitive test scores that relate to the single-parent or intact family status of the home.[198] Throughout school, in fact, black and white achievement disparities remain roughly the same, even after controlling for single-parent family status.[199] And since nearly eight in ten black children in families with incomes of $30,000 or more live with both parents, as do eighty-four percent of black children in families with $50,000 or more in annual income, the lower test scores of children in those income groups, relative to whites of even lower income families, clearly cannot be related to family structure.[200]

Although we often hear lamentations to the effect that black youth and their families simply do not place sufficient value on education (and thus their lower performance on academic indicia is not because of bias in the schools but rather their own lack of emphasis on academic pursuits), such arguments about the "lower value" placed on schooling by African Americans is little more than a racist lie. Unfortunately, this lie is in keeping with a long and ignoble tradition of blaming black culture, broadly defined, for the problems in black communities, stretching back to the infamous Coleman Report and the so-called Moynihan Report. The first, authored by sociologist James Coleman, and commissioned by Congress, and the second, authored by then-Assistant Secretary of Labor and Harvard Professor (later Senator) Daniel Patrick Moynihan, both blamed black home environments and cultural factors for everything from educational failure to out-of-wedlock pregnancy to excessive poverty rates.[201] But just as with those earlier reports, claims today that blacks simply do not place enough value on education are woefully lacking in terms of hard evidence.

First, although there are gaps in graduation rates between blacks and whites,[202] once family economic background is controlled for, blacks are actually *more likely* to finish high school than whites, and equally likely to complete college.[203] In other words, whatever differences exist in black and white educational attainment are completely the result of blacks, on average, coming from lower-income families. Comparing whites and blacks of truly similar class status reveals *greater* or equal educational attainment for blacks.

As for the degree to which blacks and whites value education—apart from the evidence of educational attainment mentioned above—black youth values are hardly different from "mainstream" white values, as any glimpse at polling and survey data of black and white youth readily demonstrates. A recent opinion poll of black youth, ages eleven to seventeen, found that the biggest hope for these youth was to go to college.[204] Additional studies have found that black youth value academic success every bit as much as white students and often place an even *higher* priority on educational achievement than whites, despite the barriers they continue to face in obtaining true equal opportunity.[205] Black tenth graders, for example, are significantly more likely than whites to discuss grades with their parents and to report that school is important to their peer group. Blacks at that age are 12.5 percent more likely than whites to say attending class is important to their friends, twenty-six percent more likely to say that studying is important to their friends, and thirty-four percent more likely than whites to say that getting good grades is important to their friends.[206]

Recently, several studies have been conducted that disprove conclusively the notion that blacks value education less than their white counterparts. An examination of longitudinal data from the 1980s and early 1990s found that blacks were just as likely as whites to aspire to college and expect to attain a college degree, that differences in dropout rates have not only been dropping but can be completely explained by economic status differences, and that contrary to the claims of many that black youth harass other blacks who do well in school for "acting white," blacks do not incur social penalties from their peers for doing well in school, any more so than students who are white.[207]

In fact, as for the "acting white" claim made so prominently by conservatives, evidence utterly undermines the legitimacy of this phenomenon as an explanation for black student performance. Studies have found that although black and Latino/a students often reject certain styles of speech, dress, and music as "acting white," they are no less likely to value behaviors conducive to educational success, such as studying, getting good grades, and making the honor roll in school.[208]

An even more recent study, conducted by the Minority Student Achievement Network (a coalition of fifteen metropolitan and urban school districts with fairly high incomes), looked at forty thousand students in seventh to eleventh grade, and found little if any evidence that blacks placed lesser value on education than their white peers. For example, according to the study, black males are more likely than white, Hispanic, or Asian males to say that it is "very important" to study hard and get good grades: indeed, white males are the *least likely* to make this claim.[209] The researchers also found that blacks were just as likely to study and work on homework as their white counterparts.[210]

This last point is backed up further by federal data, which indicate that black youth study as much as or more than white students, thereby dispelling the myth that blacks devalue learning. According to the National Center for Education Statistics, forty-three percent of black fourth graders do one hour or more of homework per night, as do forty-five percent of whites and forty-seven percent of Hispanics. In fact, black and Hispanic fourth graders are both more likely than whites that age to do more than one hour of homework, with eighteen percent of Hispanics, seventeen percent of blacks, but only fifteen percent of whites putting in this amount of study time daily.[211]

Even in high-poverty schools, disproportionately attended by inner city students of color, attitudes toward schooling are far more positive than generally believed. Students in high-poverty schools are four-and-one-half times more likely to say they have a "very positive" attitude toward academic achievement than to say they have a "very negative" attitude, and ninety-four percent of all students in such schools report a generally positive attitude toward academics—not much different from the response rate at low-poverty schools, where virtually all students report a positive attitude toward the importance of academic achievement.[212]

In fact, the evidence seems to suggest that low-income blacks are far more likely to place a high value on education than are similarly low income whites. According to research by Blau in 2003, low-income blacks are far more likely than similar whites to discuss grades with parents, to say that getting an education past high school is important to their friends, and to say that studying and getting good grades are important to their peer group.[213]

There is also no evidence that black parents take less interest in their children's education, or fail to reinforce the learning the takes place in the classroom once their children are home. Once again, statistics of National Center for Education Statistics indicate that black children are *more likely* than whites to spend time with their parents on homework. Black students are twice as likely as white students to have help from their parents on homework every day of the school week (twenty percent compared to ten percent), and while roughly half of blacks have help from parents on homework at least three times weekly, two-thirds of whites have such help twice or less, with whites a third more likely than blacks to work with parents rarely if ever on their homework.[214]

Black students also exhibit more positive attitudes and behaviors in terms of honesty and integrity. For example, blacks and Latino/as are less likely than whites to think it is okay to be late for school, to cut class, to skip school for a day, to copy someone else's homework, or to disobey and talk back to teachers. In fact, high-income whites have the *lowest* scores on measures of ethics and personal integrity, and are far more likely to endorse cheating and various forms of cutting corners to get ahead.[215]

Evidence also indicates that there is no substantial difference between white and black students in terms of whether or not their parents attend parent–teacher conferences or school meetings,[216] or ask teachers how their children are doing in class.[217] Black parents and their children are also equally likely as white children and parents to visit a library, art gallery, zoo, aquarium, museum, or historic site, as well as a community or religious event—further countering the notion that black parents take less interest in providing educational opportunities for their children.[218] Furthermore, and contrary to popular belief, most black children (about three of four) *are* read to by their parents when they are young, and are equally or more likely than whites to be taught letters, numbers, and words directly by their parents between the ages of three and five.[219] A study in 2000 by Public Agenda found that parents of color were also *more* likely than their white counterparts to stress the importance of going on to college with their kids. Two-thirds of Latino/a parents, forty-seven percent of black parents, but only thirty-three percent of white parents agreed that college was one factor that could most help a child succeed.[220]

In their groundbreaking volume, *The Source of the River*, social scientists Douglas Massey, Camille Charles, Garvey Lundy, and Mary Fischer examined longitudinal data for students of different races who were enrolled in selective colleges and universities. Their purpose was to determine the different social context in which students of color grew up as opposed to white students in these top schools, and among the issues they examined was the degree to which differential performance in college, in terms of grades, could be attributed to blacks or their families placing less value on academic performance than their white and Asian counterparts. After all, this claim has been made by some who seek to explain the persistent GPA gaps between blacks, in particular, and others in college.

Yet, as Massey and colleagues discovered, the black students had parents who were more likely than white or Asian parents to have helped them with homework growing up, more likely than white or Asian parents to have met with their teachers, equally likely to have pushed them to "do their best" in school, more likely than white parents to enroll their kids in educational camps, and equally or more likely to have participated in the PTA. Black students' parents were also more likely than parents of any other race to regularly check to make sure their kids had completed their homework and to reward their kids for good grades, while Asian parents were the *least* likely to do either of these.[221]

Likewise, the authors of this study found that black students' peers in high school had been *more likely* than white students' peers to think studying hard and getting good grades were important, and indeed white peers were the *least likely* to endorse these notions. Overall, the data suggest that if anything it is *white peer culture* that is overly dismissive of academic achievement, not black peer culture.[222]

Of all the evidence rebutting the notion that blacks place less value on education than whites, nothing makes the point more clearly than attendance information. Black twelfth graders are more than twice as likely as whites to have perfect attendance (16 percent versus 7.4 percent), and are even more likely than Asians of that age to have perfect attendance. Whites are more likely than blacks to have missed seven or more days during the last school semester, and indeed blacks are less likely than members of any racial group to have missed that many days of school in the last semester. There is also no significant difference between whites, Asians, and blacks in terms of their likelihood to skip classes,[223] a finding confirmed by independent studies as well.[224] Although the dropout rate for blacks is considerably higher than that for whites, it is still extremely small: eighty-seven percent of blacks between the ages of sixteen and twenty-four are either in school or have graduated.[225]

As a final note, while conservative critics of black "values" insist that African Americans place less value on education, as evidenced by what these critics perceive to be black behaviors and negative attitudes toward school, they are remarkably silent about the wide gaps between male and female students in terms of their attitudes toward education—gaps that are much wider, in fact, than the gaps between whites and blacks.

For example, female seniors in high school are thirty-five percent more likely than male seniors to say they "always try to do their best work," while males are 2.5 times more likely to say they seldom if ever try to do their best work. Likewise, male seniors are twice as likely as female seniors to say they often fool around in class, whereas females are nearly twice as likely as males to say they rarely or ever do so.[226] So, is the obviously greater female emphasis on education cause for condemning males as culturally pathological, or accusing them of being afraid of "acting female" by doing well in school, the way some say blacks fear "acting white" by studying hard and getting good grades? If so, why is this critique never heard among the right, and if not, why not, if the same kind of criticism is legitimate when it comes to race? And if males have indeed adopted a pathological detachment from academic excellence, why do males, as males, continue to predominate in almost all professions, earn more than their more determined and studious female counterparts, and generally escape the negative consequences of such detachment, which the right would insist have obtained for people of color?

Of course, the reason conservative critics of black "values" never critique males for their tendency to deemphasize education, or claim that men have a pathological detachment from schooling, is because such arguments—although they are far more supported by the evidence than similar claims regarding African Americans—would serve no ideological purpose in their view. Criticizing blacks, on the other hand, serves a significant ideological end, in that it encourages us to ignore the systemic barriers to equal opportunity and the litany of privileges enjoyed by whites. Instead of addressing those issues, by critiquing black families and their presumably self-destructive value systems, conservatives are able to shift the focus onto the victims of institutional racism, and blame them for their own failures to attain parity with their white counterparts. It is testimony to how entrenched racism and racist thinking are in this nation that their attempts at blaming the victims have been so successful, despite the utter lack of evidence to support their position.

4

DEFENDING
AFFIRMATIVE ACTION:
IT'S ABOUT MORE
THAN DIVERSITY

Thus far, I have examined the way racial preference continues to operate to the benefit of whites, throughout the educational system, and demonstrated how the critique of affirmative action, which holds such efforts to be unfair and harmful racial preference for people of color, is deeply flawed. The reason it has been necessary, in my estimation, to put forth such a two-pronged analysis is that, unfortunately, the biggest impediments to the future of affirmative action programs and policies are not merely the right-wing attacks launched upon it by its enemies; rather, affirmative action is also endangered by the weak defense of such efforts often put forth by its supporters.

Rarely, if ever, do we hear supporters of affirmative action discuss the institutionalized forms of white privilege and preference that remain and continue to make affirmative action necessary. In the 1996 campaign against Proposition 209 in California, for example, erstwhile defenders of affirmative action were so afraid to discuss the facts about racism and ongoing white privilege that they deliberately tried to shift the focus to gender, insisting that white women would be hurt if affirmative action were abolished. While this was true, of course, the strategy reeked of an attempt to duck the pressing and disturbing reality about racism in America. Not only was it cowardly, but ultimately this strategy also failed miserably, as it would two years later in Washington State.[1] Affirmative action is so obviously a racial issue, and opposition to it has hinged so centrally on backlash to civil rights gains and perceived white victimization, that no attempt to shift the focus from race to gender could possibly have succeeded, as was learned, the hard way, in both states.

Likewise, defenders of affirmative action in the academic realm have placed almost all of their emphasis on demonstrating the benefits of diversity, at colleges and universities especially, rather than discussing the entrenched forms of ongoing white privilege and preference that make affirmative action and "diversity" necessary. In so doing, they too have hoped to avoid the sticky, sometimes difficult discussions with which whites in particular are so uncomfortable, concerning privilege, institutional racism, and justice. Although this strategy has prevailed, for now, at the Supreme Court level (as with the University of Michigan Law School case), it remains to be seen whether emphasizing the benefits of diversity will prove to be a winning strategy in the court of public opinion. And ultimately it is that court where support will be crucial to sustaining a long-term commitment to racial equity and justice in this country.

In this concluding chapter, I briefly sketch what I consider to be the risks inherent in placing too much emphasis on the "diversity defense" as a reason for maintaining affirmative action, and demonstrate why ultimately a social justice defense, rooted in an explicit articulation of affirmative action as a necessary response to institutional racism and racial preference for whites, will be necessary to defend the concept over the long run.

I should note that I do not disagree here with the need to present the diversity defense in court, so as to protect affirmative action from legal challenge, nor do I doubt that diversity in colleges and elsewhere is a positive good. As for the first of these, because the Supreme Court has historically refused to order remedies for institutional racism (what they call "societal discrimination"[2]), I realize that making the case for affirmative action merely on the grounds that I have used in this volume would not work as a legal strategy, at least not at this time, under existing jurisprudence, and with the current makeup of the Court. As for the second of these, I think there is little doubt but that all can and do benefit from being educated in a more diverse environment and, for that matter, working in such an environment.[3] So the caveats I pose here have nothing to do with disagreement about diversity as a legal strategy or a social value; rather, they concern whether or not the diversity rationale for affirmative action is likely to work as a public rallying cry, organizing tool, or adequate defense against the ideological arguments being hurled at affirmative action by its adversaries. It is in these areas that the diversity defense, in my estimation, comes up short.

THE DIVERSITY DEFENSE IGNORES THE CONTEXT OF DIVERSITY'S ABSENCE

It is one of the great ironies of the diversity defense for affirmative action—and for that matter of all college and university programs for "enhancing diversity"—that those who espouse this principle almost never ask the fundamental question that is obviously posed by an institution's *lack* of diversity: namely, how, in a multiracial, multicultural nation, can any institution become so incredibly *nondiverse* and unrepresentative of the nation as a whole?

The diversity defense implies, whether intentionally or not, that an institution's lack of diversity just happened, as if by coincidence, or perhaps there are reasons for such a lack of diversity, but that whatever they are, we need not go into them in great detail or concern ourselves with them. In other words, the diversity defense is utterly *acontextual*, in that it ignores the reasons an institution would need to make special efforts to accomplish what we might think would happen naturally in a diverse nation. Those reasons, of course, have more than a little something to do with racism and white privilege, but because this is often left unsaid by defenders of affirmative action, the average citizen might not understand why affirmative action is needed to maintain or create diversity, whether or not it produces certain benefits. In other words, absent the proper historical and contemporary context—which is plainly that racism and white privilege have skewed opportunity to such an extent that many institutions lack meaningful diversity on the basis of race—it may prove difficult to convince people of the inherent relationship between affirmative action, on the one hand, and diversity on the other.

In fact, by ignoring the context that has led to nondiverse institutional settings, supporters of the diversity defense are essentially ceding the debate over the salience of the ongoing legacy of racism to the right. To duck this debate is to empower the conservative narrative, which says that racism and white privilege are things of the past. Whether or not this is the intention of those proffering the diversity defense is hardly relevant: this is what laypersons hear, as they would have every reason to expect supporters of affirmative action to mention ongoing racism prominently if indeed it were a serious problem. By not discussing it, racism becomes "out of sight–out of mind" and, as such, more difficult to conquer. After all, it is hard to defeat a force whose existence you barely mention.

By the same token, if the lack of diversity in an institution is itself the result of racism, past or present (or a combination of the two), then why not address that issue upfront? Doing so not only adds context to make the lack of diversity understandable; it also allows us to focus in on the root of the problem and avoid further generating a lack of diversity in institutional settings in the future.

Additionally, if, as the diversity defense argues, diversity is good because it allows people from different backgrounds and a range of experiences to learn from one another, there is still the question to be asked: Why are students' experiences so radically different in the first place, such that an increase in racial diversity would offer those students substantial new insights? The answer, of course, is obvious: It is racism itself that causes people of different races to have such radically different experiences in this society. But if that is obvious, then the benefits of diversity as a learning opportunity cannot be abstracted from the *reason* such diversity is currently lacking, and the reason people have such different backgrounds and experiences. If racism is the cause of those different experiences, and the insights that come with them, then racism, and the need to uproot it, should be sufficient rationale for affirmative action. And if ultimately the discussion leads back to racism anyway—as it does, since racism is the basis for the different experiences, from which schools hope students can learn something in a diverse setting—then why not just address the racism upfront, instead of cynically avoiding the subject?

THE DIVERSITY DEFENSE WILL NOT BOOST
SUPPORT FOR AFFIRMATIVE ACTION
AND MAY BACKFIRE

Perhaps even more importantly, basing support for affirmative action first and foremost on the benefits of diversity is a guaranteed losing strategy in the court of public opinion. Although it may be a necessary and successful strategy in courts of law, in terms of building a movement for racial equity and justice, it is almost guaranteed to fail, for a number of reasons.

First, to focus on the benefits of diversity, while downplaying or ignoring the ongoing reality of institutional racism and white privilege, appears to all who know anything about the history of these issues as a blatant retreat from earlier principles. Affirmative action was never intended to be a mechanism whereby people from different backgrounds would "learn from one another's diverse experiences," or merely reap the benefits of diverse settings. That was not the reason it was articulated, nor implemented, nor the grounds on which it was defended for the first thirty years or so of its existence. The reason for the creation of affirmative action was to help break down the barriers of institutional racism and white privilege, and to push against the "built-in headwinds" that prevented qualified and capable people of color from accessing opportunity in the job and educational markets.

To avoid now that discussion altogether, and to retreat to a diversity defense that *at best* was always secondary or tertiary to the primary purpose, is to give the impression that the original impetus no longer exists—in other words, that the reason affirmative action was created (to diminish racial inequity) is no longer necessary, perhaps because racism really has been conquered, as the right insists. As such, the diversity defense could generate widespread anger among whites who might view the supporters of affirmative action as simply shifting their argument to suit the times, or changing the reasons for affirmative action, so as to maintain so-called racial preferences in perpetuity, even though the original purpose of affirmative action has been met. Although it may seem obvious to us that the original purpose has not been met, since racism and white privilege are still quite prominent, as indicated above, unless the supporters of affirmative action are prepared to make that case, we can hardly be surprised when others do not see those issues as ongoing, and assume we are merely shifting gears for cynical purposes.

Second, and most importantly, it does not appear that support for or opposition to diversity is the key element in determining whether or not one supports affirmative action. As such, convincing people of the benefits of diversity will likely have little effect on their willingness to support affirmative action programs and policies in practical terms.

So, for example, consider the findings of practically every study ever done on the issue of the benefits of diversity. In each case, students respond to questions about their experiences with diversity on a campus, for example, and invariably and overwhelmingly respond that their experiences were positive: they feel they benefited in many ways from a diverse setting, and from learning in an environment where they were exposed to persons unlike themselves, and worked with such "others" in class or in out-of-class activities.[4] Such responses are often especially pronounced for white students, who statistically speaking were far more racially isolated before coming to college or law school.

Yet, one obvious problem immediately comes to mind when we see this kind of report, or for that matter, any other survey in which whites insist they support diversity and consider it to be of benefit: a response that most all will offer, perhaps genuinely, when asked. The problem is borne out by the countervailing survey data suggesting that whatever they may think of diversity in the abstract (or even in the concrete reality of a given institution), this does not mean those same whites will view affirmative action as a necessary component of obtaining that diversity. In other words, it is possible to support diversity and still oppose affirmative action as a mechanism for bringing diversity about. Indeed, polls consistently show that whites either oppose affirmative action outright or, at the very least, are evenly split (depending on how the question is framed),[5] which is much different from the overwhelming endorsement of diversity given by those same whites in most instances. So if support for diversity does not translate to support for affirmative action, a strategy for defending the latter which relies on cultivating the former is unlikely to make much difference. Most whites *already* believe that diversity is a good thing, but that does not cause them to support affirmative action.

Indeed, what the data quite clearly demonstrate is that the *one factor* that most dramatically separates those who support affirmative action from those who oppose it is the one factor the diversity defense proponents seem least willing to discuss, namely, the extent to which racism and discrimination against people of color are still significant problems. Those who believe they are almost invariably support affirmative action. Those who believe such things are largely behind us as a nation just as invariably oppose affirmative action.[6] In other words, what defenders of affirmative action must do, to truly affect support levels and thus build a movement for affirmative action and other racial equity measures, is to demonstrate the need for such measures, as a response to racism, which is the same reason these programs were instituted in the first place.

Although those who base their public support for affirmative action on the benefits of diversity may think they have chosen the path of least resistance—after all, as they will tell you, most people see the benefits of diversity on college campuses and even in the workplace—they have apparently mistaken the easiest, least contentious and controversial path with the one most likely to help build a movement. Just because an argument may meet with initial wide support and little resistance does not necessarily or even logically mean that the argument will lead those who accept its premises to supporting another, related argument. On the other hand, although defending affirmative action on the grounds that it is necessary to combat ongoing white privilege and institutional racism may meet with more initial resistance (and indeed it surely would), it is this argument and *only this argument* that has been demonstrated to separate the supporters from the opponents of affirmative action. So the path of greater initial resistance may be the more important path, over the long term, for building and sustaining a movement for racial equity and justice, a critical part of which is, and will remain, affirmative action.

Finally, by making the diversity defense their primary argument, some of the high-profile defenders of affirmative action (and certainly those college administrators who invariably make this the lead and, often, *only* argument they offer) are, in effect, appearing to grant one of the most pernicious of right-wing attacks against the programs, namely, the idea that students of color are indeed less qualified to attend a certain school than whites. Although few if any of the persons making the diversity argument say this openly, it is virtually impossible not to see that as the subtext of their position. After all, when the right argues that affirmative action results in lowered standards and the admission of less qualified individuals, and the liberal defenders of affirmative action respond, "Affirmative action is good because it promotes diversity, and diversity is good," what the public, understandably, hears is not only a *non sequitur*, but one that implicitly sounds like this: "Yeah, sure, they are less qualified, but hey, that's O.K., because the benefits of letting these folks into our school outweigh the costs." Unless affirmative action proponents offer a spirited rebuttal of the right-wing arguments, including a critique of the phony (and racist, and classist) merit standards the right insists upon for college admissions, they will appear to be agreeing with the right that less qualified people are getting preferences over more qualified people; and that is unlikely to strike the public as acceptable, no matter the ostensible and even quite real benefits of diversity.

THE DIVERSITY DEFENSE PREFERENCES WHITE INTERESTS AND PERSPECTIVES

Although its proponents likely do not mean for this to be the case, defending affirmative action on the basis of the benefits of diversity ultimately preferences and privileges the interests of whites over those of people of color, thereby replicating white dominance, the very thing against which affirmative action was initially arrayed. It does this in several ways.

First, advocating "diversity" as a benefit, although perfectly logical and no doubt true, replicates the dynamic that is furthered by much of the watered-down multicultural educational efforts around the country, as discussed in a previous section; namely, it "exoticizes" those who are racially different from the "norm," which is to say the dominant group, without ever interrogating the norm itself, and what it takes for granted, and how it became and remains the norm over time. In other words, the diversity defense is predicated on the notion that there are these persons out there with different experiences from the "mainstream" (although why this is so is viewed as irrelevant it seems) and different perspectives, and "we" (meaning here, the "norm") should get some of these people into our schools and workplaces, so that we can learn from them, share with them, and come to appreciate them. Never is a spotlight shone on the dominant group itself and how it came to be well positioned for so many of the best college slots and jobs in the first place. Diversity efforts become merely a mechanism for letting a few of them into our game; but make no mistake it is still our game, and we will dictate the terms of just how much change we are willing to countenance.

Second, the diversity defense almost completely ignores the issue of power, specifically, the unequal power relationship between the dominant group and those whose presence in an institution provides it with that much sought-after diversity. To read the many detailed reports defending diversity as a compelling state interest, which were submitted to the courts in the Michigan cases, is to see quite clearly the evasion of power dynamics, an evasion that clearly privileges and preferences whites by shielding them from any recognition of, or even discussion of, the ongoing imbalance of power and opportunity that works to their benefit. It is as if merely boosting the numbers of students of color, and then structuring opportunities for them to interact on a college campus, will lead to substantial growth, reductions in prejudice, and all manner of civic benefits.

Yet decades of research on the dynamics of in-group/out-group interaction and racial identity development suggest that contact alone, or contact even with substantial interaction, is insufficient to produce the desired results. Rather, interactions must take place in a context of equity, or at least a context where roughly equal power and interdependence are present.[7] Although some schools may do an excellent job of providing such opportunities for equitable interaction, we can imagine that at many other places no deliberate efforts would be made to bring about such high-level, interdependent, and equitable interaction between whites and people of color. In fact, it is quite likely that most institutions focus little on alterations in the campus climate, beyond merely "colorizing the room" with basic diversity initiatives and front-end affirmative action recruitment.[8] As such, whatever benefits could obtain under more equitable conditions might be limited, although they would surely leave in place the assumptions of entitlement to power that can so easily become prevalent in the minds of dominant group members, who have never been confronted with the injustice that brought about such disproportionate power in the first place.

Finally, and most ironically, the diversity defense often turns on its head the original notion of who affirmative action is for, and for whose benefit such efforts are being made. Whereas affirmative action initially was meant to provide qualified people of color with opportunities they would otherwise be denied, with the diversity defense affirmative action is regularly promoted as something that mostly offers benefits to whites. After all, it is whites who are most racially isolated, not students of color,[9] and thus it is whites who gain the most from diverse settings since they, more so than others, are then opened to entirely new worlds and ways of seeing things. Likewise, in corporate America, the promotion of affirmative action hiring as a way to reap the benefits of diversity is often couched in terms of how diversity makes the mostly white (but somewhat more diverse) work teams more productive, and thus the mostly white-owned companies more profitable.

Either way, it is hard not to notice that the persons for whom affirmative action is being advocated have changed dramatically. Now whites are the ones we are to be concerned about: it is *their* learning experience, *their* opportunities for personal growth, and *their* need to have *their* stereotypes countered, which comprise the justification for affirmative action. People of color, and their interests, and their needs, and their right to equal opportunity are almost entirely off the radar screen. While the benefits of diverse environments to whites are likely substantial, and even worth pointing out as an additional benefit of affirmative action efforts, it is somewhat disconcerting to see those benefits take center stage, as if affirmative action would not be defensible and justified unless the majority was getting something from it. To make white interests central to the narrative, as the diversity defense does to a large extent, is to further privilege whites and whiteness.

Even those who promote diversity because of the benefits it pays to students of color, such as Bowen and Bok, who argue that affirmative action provides people of color with opportunities to enter the nation's economic and political elite, ultimately take for granted the legitimacy of such an elite, which is going to remain white dominated, if now a bit more colorful. In other words, the power of whites is presumed to be legitimate, albeit in need of some more diversity within its ranks, so as to make that elite *more functional* and more representative, and, thus, perhaps more legitimate in the eyes of the nation and the world. However we look at it, the result is the same: the benefits to people of color are still seen as ways to benefit and maintain (and certainly never to challenge) the existing power structure. Affirmative action, in the hands of Bowen and Bok, is about helping "them" to join the power structure, not alter it.[10]

THE RIGHT WING CAN TAKE ADVANTAGE OF THE DIVERSITY DEFENSE

Then, in a move that surely should have been and could have been predicted, the diversity defense has prompted conservative critics of affirmative action to offer their own versions and visions of diversity, visions that entirely miss the point but that make perfect sense, given the acontextual, power-averse analysis of traditional liberal defenders of affirmative action. So, for example, it is not uncommon to hear conservatives insist that if racial diversity is important, so too must be "ideological diversity," and so schools should seek to hire more conservatives to traditionally left-leaning academic departments. Perhaps hire some evangelical Christians into the Women's Studies Department, or black libertarians into Ethnic Studies, or something of this nature.[11] Of course, they never extend their own logic to the conclusion that business schools should also hire Marxists, but despite this slight inconsistency, the argument is capable of gaining traction, precisely because the diversity defense, absent a discussion of the history and legacy and ongoing reality of institutional injustice, makes such arguments seem rational, and cut from the same cloth as those being used to defend affirmative action.

Now, in truth, such arguments for hiring conservatives in departments where they are underrepresented or, for that matter, trying to balance out student bodies in terms of ideological diversity as well are nothing short of absurd; but the *reason* they are absurd is what needs to be understood. The reason such positions are flawed is that Christian conservatives, for example, have never been the victims, in this country, of targeted, systemic, and institutionalized oppression and exclusion. As such, to compare their "plight" at finding jobs in the Berkeley English Literature Department, with the exclusion of instructors of color—or to compare the paucity of far-right students at Mt. Holyoke or Smith College with the paucity of students of color there, or at other elite institutions—is preposterous, because it ignores that some have been systematically excluded from opportunities and other have not. If certain academic departments have tended toward more liberal and left analyses, this is hardly because conservatives were barred from entering the disciplines in question. If evangelical Christians do not believe in Women's Studies as an academic discipline, it should hardly surprise anyone that they are scarcely found in such departments. For that matter, this is the same reason we will not find many Marxists in business schools, dedicated to training the next generation of capitalists.

In other words, once again, the issue returns to equity and opportunity: who has been afforded them and who has not, who has been excluded and who has not. This backdrop of exclusion (and its flipside, inclusion) is what makes the push for diversity necessary in the first place, for in its absence there would have been no dramatic and disproportionate overrepre-sentation of whites and underrepresentation of everyone else; no overrepresentation of men, and underrepresentation of women.

Unless we defenders of affirmative action retool our public arguments to focus principally on these justice issues, as opposed to the merely pragmatic, nuts-and-bolts benefits of diversity, opponents of affirmative action will always be able to portray themselves as equally beleaguered and equally capable of offering valuable diversity to liberal-left institutions. Although their arguments will be flawed—the reason for their inadequacy will be their lack of an injury claim, their lack of any evidence to suggest they have been the victims of systemic exclusion—if the issue is ultimately about exclusion, or lack thereof, then perhaps we would do better simply to tackle the issue where it begins, and where it almost invariably ends, instead of trying to dance around it.

Likewise, unless we make such arguments the central feature of the affirmative action defense, there will be little to prevent reactionary forces from arguing that historically black colleges and universities should also have to diversify, perhaps by admit-ting more white students. Even though no such schools ever discriminated against whites on the basis of race, and although whites were always welcome to attend such institutions, unless the diversity discussion is rooted in an understanding of who has and who has not been the victim of systemic exclusion, it will be hard to defend against such absurd permutations as this.

It is at times like these, as difficult as it is to say, that we might do well to remember the words of Ronald Reagan. After all, it was Reagan, who as governor of the State of California, signed into law a broad array of affirmative action programs, most of which were done away with in 1996 thanks to Proposition 209. And it was Reagan who explained his actions at the time in the following way:

> Time and experience have shown that laws and edicts of nondiscrimination are not enough. Justice demands that each and every citizen consciously adopt and accentuate a real and personal commitment to affirmative action, so as to make equal opportunity a reality.[12]

Certainly, the supporters of racial equity and justice should be willing to sound at least as progressive, and should be expected to be at least as bold in their pronouncements, as Reagan, who in spite of his administration's attacks on affirmative action beginning in the 1980s, had, at one time, seen the value of such efforts in terms that were explicitly about equal opportunity.

In the final analysis, affirmative action remains important and necessary because racism remains prevalent and damaging to the life prospects of people of color in the United States. It remains necessary because white privilege and white racial preferences, in all areas of national life, remain ubiquitous. The history of this nation is the history of affirmative action, for white people. Until that affirmative action and its ongoing legacy are eradicated, all talk of ending the programs we tend to think of when we hear the term is not only premature but a call for the permanent institutionalization of white supremacy in America. We owe future generations better than that.

NOTES

NOTES TO CHAPTER ONE

1. Fred L. Pincus, *Reverse Discrimination: Dismantling the Myth* (Boulder, Colo.: Lynne Rienner Publishers, 2003), 21–27.
2. Ibid., 24–25.
3. Barbara R. Bergmann, *In Defense of Affirmative Action* (New York: Basic Books, 1996), 44.
4. *Review of Federal Affirmative Action Programs: Report to the President* (Washington, D.C.: U.S. Government Printing Office, 1995), sec. 6.
5. Ibid.
6. Ibid.
7. Martin Luther King, Jr., *Why We Can't Wait* (New York: Harper & Row, 1963). We would hope that this quote from King, as well as several others made in his lifetime, would put to rest the mistaken notion that he would have opposed affirmative action. This argument has been made prominently by many conservatives, including Ward Connerly, Dinesh D'Souza, Abigail and Stephan Thernstrom, and Clint Bolick, despite the clear evidence of King's support for such efforts. See Tim Wise, "Misreading the Dream: The Truth About Martin Luther King Jr. and Affirmative Action," *LIP Magazine* (January 20, 2003).

8. Michael K. Brown et al., *Whitewashing Race: The Myth of a Color-Blind Society* (Berkeley: University of California, 2003), 167.
9. *Griggs v. Duke Power Co.*, 401 U.S. 424 (1971).
10. Brown et al., *Whitewashing Race*, 167.
11. Bergmann, *In Defense of Affirmative Action*, 72–74, 79.
12. Stephanie A. Goodwin, "Situational Power and Interpersonal Dominance Facilitate Bias and Inequality," *Journal of Social Issues* (Winter 1998).
13. Alice O'Connor et al., *The Multi-City Study of Urban Inequality: Urban Inequality: Evidence From Four Cities* (New York: Russell Sage Foundation, 1999); Bergmann, *In Defense of Affirmative Action*, 70.
14. Gertrude Ezorsky, *Racism and Justice: The Case for Affirmative Action* (Ithaca, N.Y.: Cornell University Press, 1991).
15. Edward W. Jones, Jr., "Black Managers: The Dream Deferred," in *Differences That Work: Organizational Excellence Through Diversity*, ed. Mary C. Gentile (Cambridge, Mass.: Harvard Business School Press, January 1994), 65, 74–75.
16. Marc Bendick, Charles W. Jackson, and Victor Reinoso, "Measuring Employment Discrimination Through Controlled Experiments," *Review of Black Political Economy* 25 (Summer 1994).
17. LeAnn Lodder et al., *Racial Preference and Suburban Employment Opportunities* (Chicago: Legal Assistance Foundation of Metropolitan Chicago and the Chicago Urban League, April 2003).
18. Philip Moss and Chris Tilly, *Stories Employers Tell: Race, Skill and Hiring in America* (New York: Russell Sage Foundation, 2001).
19. O'Connor et al., *Multi-City Study of Urban Inequality*.
20. Brown et al., *Whitewashing Race*, 84–85.
21. Stephen Steinberg, "Occupational Apartheid in America," in *Without Justice for All*, ed. Adolph Reed, Jr. (Boulder, Colo.: Westview Press, 1999), 224.
22. Moss and Tilly, *Stories Employers Tell*, 106.
23. M. Bertrand and S. Mullainathan, "Are Emily and Brendan More Employable than Lakisha and Jamal? A Field Experiment on Labor Market Discrimination." Available online at http://gsb.uchicago.edu/pdf/bertrand.pdf, November 18, 2002; Alan B. Krueger, "What's in a Name? Plenty If You're a Job-Seeker," *New York Times*, December 12, 2002.
24. Devah Pager, "The Mark of a Criminal Record," *American Journal of Sociology* 108, 5 (March 2003): 937–75.

25. Sally Lehrman, "Why Race-Based Data Matters," *AlterNet*. Available online at http://www.alternet.org.print.html?StoryID=16912 (October 6, 2003).

26. Brown et al., *Whitewashing Race*, 36.

27. Tom W. Smith, "Ethnic Images," General Social Survey (GSS) Technical Report 19 (Chicago: National Opinion Research Center, January 1991).

28. Shana Levin, "Social Psychological Evidence on Race and Racism," in *Compelling Interest: Examining the Evidence on Racial Dynamics in Colleges and Universities*, ed. Mitchell J. Chang et al. (Palo Alto, Calif.: Stanford University Press, 2003), 99.

29. William M. Hartnett, "Income Gaps Persist Among Races," *Palm Beach Post*, October 20, 2003.

30. Patrick L. Mason, "Race, Cognitive Ability, and Wage Inequality," *Challenge* (May–June, 1998).

31. Hartnett, "Income Gaps Persist Among Races."

32. Linda Faye Williams, *The Constraint of Race: Legacies of White Skin Privilege* (University Park: Pennsylvania State University Press, 2003), 359, fig. 7.1.

33. U.S. Bureau of the Census, Survey of Income and Program Participation, unpublished data, April 2001, in U.S. Department of Education, National Center for Education Statistics, *Digest of Education Statistics* (Washington, D.C.: U.S. Government Printing Office, 2001), table 10:19.

34. U.S. Department of Education, National Center for Education Statistics, *The Condition of Education* (Washington, D.C.: U.S. Government Printing Office, 1994).

35. U.S. Bureau of the Census, Survey of Income, table 10:19.

36. Ibid.

37. Gordon E. Samson et al., "Academic and Occupational Performance: A Quantitative Synthesis," *American Educational Research Journal* 21 (1984): 311–21.

38. Mason, *Race, Cognitive Ability*.

39. William G. Bowen and Derek Bok, *The Shape of the River: Long Term Consequences of Considering Race in College and University Admissions* (Princeton, N.J.: Princeton University Press, 1998), 259.

40. Pincus, *Reverse Discrimination*, 18.

41. Carl Rowan, *The Coming Race War in America* (New York: Little Brown, 1996), 130.

42. Brown et al., *Whitewashing Race*, 189.

43. Melvin Oliver and Thomas Shapiro, *Black Wealth, White Wealth: A New Perspective on Racial Inequality* (New York: Routledge, 1996).

44. Edward S. Herman, "America the Meritocracy," *Z Magazine* (July/August 1996).

45. *Civil Rights Cases* 109 U.S. 3 (1883).

46. Philip F. Rubio, *A History of Affirmative Action, 1619–2000* (Jackson: University Press of Mississippi, 2001), 40.

47. Seventy-eight percent of whites in 2000 said this. Howard Schuman et al., "Recent Trends in Racial Attitudes: A 2002 Data Update for the 1997 Book, *Racial Attitudes in America: Trends and Interpretations*" (Cambridge, Mass.: Harvard University Press, 2002). Available online at http://tigger.cc.uic.edu/~krysan/racialattitudes.htm.

48. Noel Ignatiev, *How the Irish Became White* (New York: Routledge, 1994); Karen Brodkin, *How the Jews Became White Folks: And What That Says About Race in America* (Brunswick, N.J.: Rutgers University Press, 1994); Jennifer Guglielmo and Salvatore Salerno, eds., *Are Italians White? How Race Is Made in America* (New York: Routledge, 2003).

49. Rubio, *History of Affirmative Action*, 5.

50. A. Leon Higginbotham, *In the Matter of Color: Race and the American Legal Process—The Colonial Period* (New York: Oxford University Press, 1980); Rubio, *History of Affirmative Action*.

51. Herbert Gutman and the American Social History Project, *Who Built America? Working People and the Nation's Economy, Politics, Culture and Society*, Vol. 1 (New York: Pantheon, 1989), 518.

52. Rubio, *History of Affirmative Action*.

53. For detailed analyses of the FHA and VA loan programs and how they discriminated racially, see Douglas Massey and Nancy Denton, *American Apartheid: Segregation and the Making of the Underclass* (Cambridge, Mass.: Harvard University, 1993); Oliver and Shapiro, *Black Wealth, White Wealth*.

54. Brown et al., *Whitewashing Race*, 77.

55. Leonard Steinhorn and Barbara Diggs-Brown, *By the Color of Our Skin: The Illusion of Integration and the Reality of Race* (New York: Dutton, 1999), 95–96.

56. Jill Quadagno, *The Color of Welfare: How Racism Undermined the War on Poverty* (New York: Oxford University Press, 1994), 91; Brown et al., *Whitewashing Race*.

57. Brown et al., *Whitewashing Race*, 78.

58. George Lipsitz, *The Possessive Investment in Whiteness: How Whites Profit from Identity Politics* (Philadelphia: Temple University Press, 1998), 6–7.
59. Micaela di Leonardo, "'Why Can't They Be Like Our Grandparents?' and Other Radical Fairytales," in *Without Justice for All*, ed. Adolph Reed (Boulder, Colo.: Westview Press, 1999), 42.
60. Massey and Denton, *American Apartheid*, 200.
61. Ibid., 85.
62. Oliver and Shapiro, *Black Wealth, White Wealth*.
63. Edward N. Wolff, *Recent Trends in Wealth Ownership, 1983–1998* (Levy Economics Institute of Bard College, Working Paper 300, April 2000), 9; Robert Avery and Michael Rendall, "Lifetime Inheritances of Three Generations of Whites and Blacks," *American Journal of Sociology* 107, 5 (March 2002).
64. Shawna Orzechowski and Peter Sepielli, *Net Worth and Asset Ownership of Households: 1998 and 2000* (Washington, D.C.: U.S. Bureau of the Census, Current Population Reports, P70-88, May 2003), 2.
65. Dalton Conley, *Being Black, Living in the Red* (Berkeley: University of California Press, 1999).
66. Maria Krysan, "Recent Trends in Racial Attitudes." Available online at http://tigger.cc.uic.edu (2002).
67. Gary Orfield and Susan Eaton, *Dismantling Desegregation: The Quiet Reversal of Brown v. Board of Education* (New York: New Press, 1996), 27.
68. Donald R. Kinder and Lynn M. Sanders, *Divided by Color: Racial Politics and Democratic Ideals* (Chicago: University of Chicago Press, 1996), 7, 21, 134.
69. Pincus, *Reverse Discrimination*, 7.
70. Ibid., 89–109.
71. Paul Burstein, "Reverse Discrimination Cases in Federal Courts: Legal Mobilization by a Counter-movement," *Sociological Quarterly* 32 (1991): 511–28.

NOTES TO CHAPTER TWO

1. Judith R. Blau, *Race in the Schools: Perpetuating White Dominance?* (Boulder, Colo.: Lynne Rienner Press, 2003), 48.
2. Christopher Shea, "Back to School," *Washington Post*, July 22, 2001.

3. Alfie Kohn, *Punished by Rewards: The Trouble with Gold Stars, Incentive Plans, A's, Praise, and Other Bribes* (Boston: Houghton Mifflin, 1999), 117.

4. Schuman et al., "Recent Trends in Racial Attitudes."

5. Kohn, *Punished by Rewards*, 111.

6. James Waller, *Face to Face: The Changing State of Racism Across America* (New York: Insight Books, 1998), 144; Valerie E. Lee and David T. Burkam, *Inequality at the Starting Gate: Social Background Differences in Achievement as Children Begin School* (Washington, DC: Economic Policy Institute, 2002).

7. Willie Legette, "The Crisis of the Black Male: New Ideology in Black Politics," in *Without Justice for All*, ed. Adolph Reed, Jr. (Boulder, Colo.: Westview Press, 1999), 305.

8. Blau, *Race in the Schools*, 204.

9. U.S. Department of Education, *Digest of Education Statistics*, 121, table 98.

10. John Yinger, *Closed Doors, Opportunities Lost: The Continuing Costs of Housing Discrimination* (New York: Russell Sage Foundation, 1995), 138.

11. Ibid., 139.

12. Ibid.

13. U.S. Department of Education, *Digest of Education Statistics*, 121, table 98.

14. Gary Orfield et al., "Deepening Segregation in American Public Schools: A Special Report From the Harvard Project on School Desegregation," *Equity & Excellence in Education* 30 (1997): 5–24.

15. Massey and Denton, *American Apartheid*, 153.

16. Ibid., 85.

17. Oliver and Shapiro, *Black Wealth, White Wealth*.

18. Massey and Denton, *American Apartheid*, 153.

19. U.S. Department of Education, National Center for Education Statistics, *The Condition of Education 2002* (Washington, D.C.: U.S. Government Printing Office, 2002), 58.

20. Valerie Martinez-Ebers, "Latino Interests in Education, Health and Criminal Justice Policy," *Political Science and Politics* (September 2000).

21. Stephen J. Ceci, "How Much Does Schooling Influence General Intelligence and Its Cognitive Components? A Reassessment of the Evidence," *Developmental Psychology* 27 (1991): 703–22.

22. Amanda E. Lewis, *Race in the Schoolyard: Negotiating the Color Line in Classrooms and Communities* (New Brunswick, N.J.: Rutgers University Press, 2003), 120.

23. Ibid., 88.

24. Charmaine Llagas, *Status and Trends in the Education of Hispanics* (Washington, D.C.: U.S. Department of Education, National Center for Education Statistics, 2003), 148, suppl. table 4.2c; U.S. Department of Education, *The Condition of Education 2002*, 56.

25. Claude S. Fischer et al., *Inequality by Design: Cracking the Bell Curve Myth* (Princeton, N.J.: Princeton University Press, 1996), 163.

26. Stephen Thernstrom and Abigail Thernstrom, *America in Black and White: One Nation, Indivisible* (New York: Simon & Schuster, 1997).

27. Kevin Carey, *The Funding Gap: Low Income and Minority Students Still Receive Fewer Dollars in Many States* (Washington, D.C.: The Education Trust, 2003).

28. David C. Berliner and Bruce J. Biddle, *The Manufactured Crisis: Myths, Fraud, and the Attack on America's Public Schools* (Reading, Mass.: Addison-Wesley, 1995), 264–65; Jonathan Kozol, *Savage Inequalities* (New York: Crown Books, 1991).

29. U.S. General Accounting Office, "School Finance: State Efforts to Reduce Funding Gaps Between Poor and Wealthy Districts," *Letter Report* (February 5, 1997).

30. Ibid.

31. Applied Research Center, ERASE Fact Sheet, "Public Schools in the United States: Still Separate, Still Unequal" (Oakland, Calif.: Applied Research Center, 2000).

32. Linda Darling-Hammond, "Unequal Opportunity: Race and Education," *Brookings Review* (Spring 1998): 31.

33. Brown et al., *Whitewashing Race*, 111.

34. Jawanza Kunjufu, *Black Students, Middle Class Teachers* (Chicago: African American Images, 2002), 57.

35. Ibid., 58.

36. Orfield and Eaton, *Dismantling Desegregation*, 69.

37. Dinesh D'Souza, *The End of Racism: Principles for a Multiracial Society* (New York: The Free Press, 1995); Thernstrom and Thernstrom, *America in Black and White*.

38. Orfield and Eaton, *Dismantling Desegregation*, 86–87.

39. Patrick J. Finn, *Literacy With an Attitude: Educating Working-Class Children in Their Own Self-Interest* (Albany, N.Y.: SUNY Press, 1999), 32–36.

40. Trial Testimony of Martin Shapiro in *Grutter v. Bollinger et al.*, 97-75928 E.D. Mich. (February 6, 2001).
41. Rebecca Gordon, *Education and Race* (Oakland, Calif.: Applied Research Center, 1998), 48–49.
42. Fischer et al., *Inequality by Design*, 164–65.
43. Steinhorn and Diggs-Brown, *By the Color of Our Skin*, 47.
44. Orfield and Eaton, *Dismantling Desegregation*, 68.
45. Llagas, *Status and Trends*, 157, suppl. table 4.7.
46. Richard Whitmire, "Few Black Students Taking Advanced Placement Classes," *Nashville Tennessean*, June 2, 2000.
47. Asian Law Caucus, "Facts and Fantasies About UC Berkeley Admissions: A Critical Evaluation of Regent John Moores' Report" (Berkeley, Calif.: Asian Law Caucus, October 24, 2003).
48. Jeannie Oakes, *Keeping Track: How Schools Structure Inequality* (New Haven, Conn.: Yale University Press, 1985), 11.
49. Kohn, *Punished by Rewards*, 107.
50. Oakes, *Keeping Track*, 169.
51. Ibid., 175.
52. Ibid., 8–9.
53. Blau, *Race in the Schools*, 137.
54. Oakes, *Keeping Track*, 8–11.
55. Ibid., 101.
56. Asian Law Caucus, "Facts and Fantasies"; Whitmire, "Few Black Students."
57. Jawanza Kunjufu, *Countering the Conspiracy to Destroy Black Boys* (Chicago: African American Images, 1995), 47.
58. Robert C. Smith, *Racism in the Post-Civil Rights Era: Now You See It, Now You Don't* (Albany, N.Y.: SUNY Press, 1995), 26.
59. U.S. Department of Education *The Condition of Education 2002*, 180, table 30-3; 45.
60. Lewis, *Race in the Schoolyard*, 49.
61. Ronald F. Ferguson, "Teacher's Perceptions and Expectations and the Black–White Test Score Gap," in *The Black–White Test Score Gap*, ed. Christopher Jencks and Meredith Phillips (Washington, D.C.: Brookings Institution Press, 1998), 281.
62. Kunjufu, *Black Students, Middle Class Teachers*, 96.
63. Ibid., 98.
64. Blau, *Race in the Schools*, 55.
65. Lewis, *Race in the Schoolyard*.
66. Paul Tosto, "When Race, Discipline Meet," *St Paul Pioneer Press*, May 6, 2002.

67. Russell J. Skiba et al., *The Color of Discipline: Sources of Racial and Gender Disproportionality in School Punishment* (Indiana Education Policy Center, Policy Research Report SRS1, June 2000), 4.

68. Ibid., 6, 13.

69. U.S. Centers for Disease Control and Prevention, *Youth Risk Behavior Surveillance System: Youth 2003 Online, Comprehensive Results* (2004). Available online at http://apps.nccd.cdc.gov/yrbss.

70. Jill DeVoe et al., *Indicators of School Crime and Safety: 2002* (Washington, D.C.: U.S. Departments of Education and Justice, November 2002), 8.

71. Ibid.

72. P. Kaufman et al., *Indicators of School Crime and Safety: 2001* (Washington, D.C.: U.S. Departments of Education and Justice, October 2001).

73. Skiba et al., *The Color of Discipline*, 11.

74. Ibid., 17.

75. Michael Winerip, "In the Affluent Suburbs, an Invisible Race Gap," *New York Times*, June 4, 2003.

76. James W. Loewen, *Lies My Teacher Told Me: Everything Your American History Textbook Got Wrong* (New York: New Press, 1995).

77. Julie Kailin, *Antiracist Education: From Theory to Practice* (New York: Rowman & Littlefield, 2002); "Taking Multicultural, Anti-Racist Education Seriously: An Interview with Enid Lee," in *Rethinking Schools: An Agenda for Change*, ed. David Levine et al. (New York: New Press, 1995), 9–16; Lewis, *Race in the Schoolyard*, 17; Louise Derman-Sparks, "How Well Are We Nurturing Ethnic Diversity," in *Rethinking Schools: An Agenda for Change*, ed. David Levine et al. (New York: New Press, 1995), 17–22.

78. U.S. Department of Education, *The Condition of Education 2002*, 188, table 33-1.

79. Expert Report of Tim Wise, Submitted in *Gwen and Odell Thomas et al. v. Puyallup School District et al.* W.D. Wash. (March 2001).

80. Lewis, *Race in the Schoolyard*, 19.

NOTES TO CHAPTER THREE

1. Goodwin Liu, "The Myth and Math of Affirmative Action," *Washington Post*, April 14, 2002.

2. Mary Beth Marklein, "Two White Students Sue Over Entry Policies," *USA Today*, October 15, 1997.

3. Pincus, *Reverse Discrimination*, 50.

4. *New Orleans Times-Picayune*, May 21, 1995; Lydia Chavez, *The Color Bind: California's Battle to End Affirmative Action* (Berkeley: University of California Press, 1998), 14.

5. Roberta J. Hill, "Far More Than Frybread," in *Race in the College Classroom: Pedagogy and Politics*, ed. Bonnie TuSmith and Maureen T. Reddy (New Brunswick, N.J.: Rutgers University Press), 169.

6. Llagas, *Status and Trends*, 170, suppl. table 7.7.

7. Caroline Sotello, Viernes Turner, and Samuel L. Myers, Jr., "Faculty Diversity and Affirmative Action," in *Affirmative Action's Testament of Hope: Strategies for a New Era in Higher Education*, ed. Mildred Garcia (Albany, N.Y.: SUNY Press, 1997), 131–48.

8. Thomas J. Kane and William T. Dickens, "Racial and Ethnic Preferences in College Admissions," Policy Brief 9 (Washington, D.C.: Brookings Institution, November 1996).

9. Anthony Carnevale and Stephen J. Rose, *Socioeconomic Status, Race/Ethnicity and Selective College Admissions* (New York: Century Foundation, 2003), 7–10.

10. Liu, "Myth and Math."

11. Sylvia Hurtado and Christine Navia, "Reconciling College Access and the Affirmative Action Debate," in *Affirmative Action's Testament of Hope*, ed. Mildred Garcia (Albany, N.Y.: SUNY Press, 1997), 115.

12. Rubio, *History of Affirmative Action*, 183.

13. William Trent et al., "Justice, Equality of Educational Opportunity, and Affirmative Action in Higher Education," in *Compelling Interest: Examining the Evidence on Racial Dynamics in Colleges and Universities*, ed. Mitchell J. Chang et al. (Palo Alto, Calif.: Stanford University Press, 2003), 46.

14. J. F. Dovidio and S. L. Gaertner, "Affirmative Action, Unintentional Racial Biases, and Intergroup Relations," *Journal of Social Issues* 52, 4 (1996): 51–75.

15. Carnevale and Rose, *Socioeconomic Status, Race/Ethnicity*, 25.

16. D. Solorzano "The Baccalaureate Origins of Chicana and Chicano Doctorates in the Social Sciences," *Hispanic Journal of Behavioral Sciences* 17 (1995): 3–32; D. Solórzano, "The Doctorate Production and Baccalaureate Origins of African Americans in the Sciences and Engineering," *Journal of Negro Education* 64 (1995): 15–32; D. Solórzano and Associates, *The Design of an Information System for the UCLA Academic Advancement Program: A Report to the University of California, Los Angeles* (1994).

17. U.S. General Accounting Office, "Information on Minority Targeted Scholarships," B251634 (Washington, D.C.: U.S. Government Printing Office, January 1994).

18. Stephen L. Carter, "Color-Blind and Color-Active," *The Recorder*, January 3, 1992.

19. Ronald J. Fiscus, *The Constitutional Logic of Affirmative Action: Making the Case for Quotas* (Durham, N.C.: Duke University Press, 1992), 38–39.

20. Joel Dreyfuss and Charles Lawrence III, *The Bakke Case: The Politics of Inequality* (New York: Harcourt, Brace, Jovanovich, 1979).

21. Charles Lawrence III and Mari Matsuda, *We Won't Go Back: Making the Case for Affirmative Action* (New York: Houghton-Mifflin, 1997), 44; Alphonso Pinkney, *The Myth of Black Progress* (New York: Cambridge University Press, 1984), 153–54.

22. Lipsitz, *Possessive Investment in Whiteness*, 36.

23. Liu, "Myth and Math."

24. Mark Acosta, "King's Name for School Draws Fire: Some Parents Fear Bias by Colleges, Others Want to Honor Citrus Heritage," *Riverside Press-Enterprise*, January 3, 1998.

25. Brief for Respondents, In the Supreme Court of the United States, *Jennifer Gratz et al. v. Lee Bollinger et al.* Available online at www.umich.edu/~urel/admissions/legal/gratz/UM-Gratz.pdf (2003), 1.

26. Ibid., 2, fn.

27. Ibid., 7

28. Ibid., 8

29. Ibid.

30. Ibid.

31. Carnevale and Rose, *Socioeconomic Status, Race/Ethnicity*, 37.

32. Brief for Respondents, 8.

33. Liu, "Myth and Math."

34. Trial Testimony of Kinley Larntz, in *Grutter v. Bollinger et al.*, 97-75928 E.D. Mich. (February 10, 2001).

35. Ibid., 85.

36. Law School Admissions Council, *What Is a Score Band?* (Law School Admissions Council, 1997).

37. Expert Report of David M. White, submitted in *Grutter v. Bollinger et al.*, 97-75928 E.D. Mich. (2001).

38. Ibid., 23.

39. Karin Chenoweth, "Puzzling Percentiles," *Washington Post*, October 25, 1998.

40. Expert Report of David M. White, 27.
41. Ibid.
42. Trial Testimony of Steven W. Raudenbush, in *Grutter v. Bollinger et al.*, 97-75928 E.D. Mich. vol. 4 (January 19, 2001).
43. "Information on Admissions Lawsuits—U. of Michigan." Available online at www.umich.edu/~urel/admissions/faqs.
44. Expert Report of David M. White.
45. Rene Sanchez, "With Ban on Preferences, UC Will Enroll 12% Fewer Blacks, Hispanics," *Washington Post*, May 21, 1998.
46. Asian Law Caucus, "Facts and Fantasies." Indeed, a study by the University of California of 78,000 freshmen who entered the UC system between 1996 and 1999 found that high school GPA explained 15.4 percent of the difference in freshmen grades, and high school GPA combined with SAT scores only explained 20.8 percent of the difference in freshman grades. Thus, the SAT adds a mere 5.4 percentage points to the predictive validity of high school GPA alone.
47. "Cadet Quotas," *Savannah Now* (Savannah Morning News, Electronic Edition), June 5, 1998.
48. William T. Dickens and Thomas J. Kane, "Racial Test Score Differences as Evidence of Reverse Discrimination: Less Than Meets the Eye," *Industrial Relations* 38 (July 1999): 331–57.
49. Joseph L. Graves, Jr., *The Emperor's New Clothes: Biological Theories of Race at the Millennium* (New Brunswick, N.J.: Rutgers University Press, 2001), 164.
50. Claude Steele, "Understanding the Performance Gap," in *Who's Qualified?* ed. Lani Guinier and Susan Sturm (Boston: Beacon Press, 2001), 64.
51. National Commission on Fair and Open Testing, "The SAT: Questions and Answers—A Fact Sheet." Available online at www.fairtest. org/facts/satfact.htm.
52. Berliner and Biddle, *The Manufactured Crisis*, 16.
53. Richard Nisbett, "Blue Genes," *The New Republic* (October 31, 1994). Interestingly, research shows that coaching on the SAT has a particularly dramatic effect on black scores. This is important for two reasons. First, it demonstrates that the test has little to do with innate ability or aptitude on the part of blacks, since if it did measure such things, coaching could have little impact. Second, it demonstrates the interrelationship between the race and class bias of such tests. Because blacks are disproportionately from lower-income families, their inability to afford coaching classes means that despite

the benefit of such coaching, it will remain off limits for far too many students of color. See Beverly P. Cole, "College Admissions & Coaching," in *Testing African American Students*, ed. Asa Hilliard (Chicago: Third World Press, 1991), 103–4.

54. Ishmael Reed, "African Americans Outpropagandized Again," *The Black Scholar* (Summer 1995). Reports are increasingly common of wealthy white parents in affluent communities "shopping" for doctors willing to diagnose (for a price) their children as learning disabled. Such a diagnosis allows a student to receive extra time on the SAT, thereby substantially reducing the pressures otherwise associated with a timed test. Though such parents hardly sought a learning disabled label for their children in school—after all, such a label would have hardly helped land their kids coveted slots in honors and advanced placement classes—when it comes test time, these parents have shown themselves willing to cut any corners necessary to preserve their children's privileged status. David Callahan, *The Cheating Culture: Why More Americans are Doing Wrong to Get Ahead* (Orlando, Fla.: Harcourt, Inc., 2004), 8, 211, 228.

55. Berliner and Biddle, *The Manufactured Crisis*, 19.

56. Carnevale and Rose, *Socioeconomic Status, Race/Ethnicity*, 28.

57. This statistic is from the College Board's Handbook for the SAT Program 2000–2001, which notes that the maximum correlation between SAT verbal and math tests on the one hand and freshman grades in college on the other is 0.47 and 0.48, respectively. Because correlations are squared to determine the predictive validity of a given factor between two other factors (here, grades between two different freshmen), the explanatory value is roughly 0.22. FairTest, "SAT I: A Faulty Instrument for Predicting College Success" (Cambridge, Mass.: National Center for Fair and Open Testing, 2002).

58. Linda Wightman, "Standardized Testing and Equal Access: A Tutorial," in *Compelling Interest: Examining the Evidence on Racial Dynamics in Colleges and Universities*, ed. Mitchell J. Chang et al. (Palo Alto, Calif.: Stanford University Press, 2003), 67. This statistic comes from squaring the mean correlation coefficient (0.42) as offered in Wightman, citing several different studies. Also see Peter McLaren, "White Supremacy and the Politics of Fear and Loathing," in *Measured Lies: The Bell Curve Examined*, ed. Joe L. Kinchloe, Shirley R. Steinberg, and Aaron Gresson III (New York: St. Martin's Press, 1997), 361; Graves, *The Emperor's New Clothes*, 164. Supporters of standardized testing argue that this kind of criticism is unfair, in that correlation

coefficients between test scores and first-year grades are only this low due to something called "range restriction." Range restriction refers to the fact that at most schools (especially selective ones) the range of persons admitted is already limited in terms of scores and prior grades, since scores and grades are part of the formula used to select students in the first place. In other words, obviously the impact on performance won't seem large because, for the most part, all students admitted had done pretty well on prior tests; but, they insist, if the students who scored badly had been accepted, the correlation would have been very high, as the low-scoring students would have tended to do far worse in class. Essentially, they are arguing that the test itself is valid, and if less qualified people were admitted to certain schools, the correlation would grow dramatically. There are many statisticians who question the validity of this critique, noting that the range of applicants is not random, but rather all from students with a plausible chance of succeeding, especially at elite schools, and so the correlation "corrections" that try to predict how low scorers would have done are absurd, since truly low scorers wouldn't have applied to such schools in the first place, at least not in large numbers. Truly bad students, in other words, simply don't apply to Harvard, so to suggest that the SAT would be highly correlated with grades if Harvard let in hundreds of kids with scores below 1000 (on a 1600 point scale) is utterly irrelevant. Furthermore, even as the defenders of testing (and those who make the range restriction argument) point out, those persons who are admitted with relatively low scores or grades, or who would be if affirmative action were intensified, are likely to be students with other elements of "merit" to recommend them to a particular school. No defender of affirmative action, after all, is calling for purely open admissions, with no reference to academic merit indicia. So if some students with lower scores are admitted, because perhaps the school considered race and how race might well have affected an applicant's prior opportunities, they would not be getting the same kind of student as the "typical" student with that same low score. Thus, the relationship to future grades between that applicant's score of 1000, for example, might be lower than the correlation for a comparable white applicant with a score of 1000. As a result, correcting for range restriction may be inappropriate, since the persons not admitted who might have been under different criteria would not differ all that much from the applicants who were admitted.

59. FairTest, "SAT I."

60. Susan Sturm and Lani Guinier, "Affirmative Action: Reclaiming the Innovative Ideal," *California Law Review* 84 (1996): 953, available online at http://www.law.upenn.edu/racetalk/reprint.htm; Cole (1991), 101; Peter Schonemann, "Transcript: Race, Genes, and Intelligence" (New York: The Gene Media Forum, March 21, 2002).

61. FairTest, "SAT I."

62. Gregg Thomson, "Is the SAT a 'Good Predictor' of Graduation Rates?" (Berkeley: University of California, Office of Student Research, 1999). For example, among those entering Berkeley in 1988, there was almost no difference in graduation rates for students, whether they had scored below 1000 or above 1500. Specifically, once recruited athletes admitted despite lower academic credentials are excluded from the analysis, those with SATs between 900 and 999 graduated at a rate of seventy-nine percent, hardly different from the eighty-two percent rate at which students who scored between 1500 and 1599 graduated. Even those who scored between 800 and 899 graduated seventy-five percent of the time, and those scoring between 1000 and 1099 graduated at the same rate as those scoring between 1500 and 1599.

63. FairTest, "SAT I."

64. John G. Weiss, "It's Time to Examine the Examiners," in *Testing African American Students*, ed. Asa Hilliard III (Chicago: Third World Press, 1991), 89.

65. Lani Guinier and Susan Sturm, "Reply," in *Who's Qualified?* eds. Lani Guinier and Susan Sturm (Boston: Beacon Press, 2001), 99.

66. University of Texas Admissions Research. Available online at www.utexas.edu/student/research/reports/admissions.

67. FairTest, "The ACT: Biased, Inaccurate, Coachable and Misused" (Cambridge, Mass.: National Commission for Fair and Open Testing, 2002). Available online at www.fairtest.org/facts/act.html.

68. Ibid.

69. Cecilia A. Conrad, "Affirmative Action and Admission to the University of California," in *Impacts of Affirmative Action: Policies & Consequences in California*, ed. Paul Ong (Walnut Grove, Calif.: AltaMira Press, 1999).

70. Douglas Massey, Camille Charles, Garvey Lundy, and Mary Fischer, *The Source of the River: The Social Origins of Freshmen at America's Selective Colleges and Universities* (Princeton, N.J.: Princeton Univeristy Press, 2003).

71. Ibid., 82.
72. Carnevale and Rose, *Socioeconomic Status, Race/Ethnicity*, 36–37.
73. Weiss (1991), 87.
74. Greg Tanaka, "Dysgenesis and White Culture," in *Measured Lies: The Bell Curve Examined*, ed. Joe L. Kinchloe, Shirley R. Steinberg, and Aaron D. Gresson (New York: St. Martin's Press, 1997), 305.
75. Linda Wightman, "The Threat to Diversity in Legal Education: An Empirical Analysis of the Consequences of Abandoning Race as a Factor in Law School Admission Decisions," 72 *New York University Law Review* 1 (April, 1997): 32. As with the SAT, here too, defenders of standardized testing argue that the relatively low correlations are due to range restriction; and as with the SAT, the range restriction argument is subject to the same rebuttal as proffered previously in footnote 58. Importantly, it should be noted that schools with substantial affirmative action policies appear to demonstrate lower correlations between LSAT scores and first-year law school grades (Lisa C. Anthony, Vincent F. Hams, and Peter J. Pashley, *Predictive Validity of the LSAT: A National Summary of the 1995–1996 Correlation Studies*, Newtown, Penn.: Law School Admission Council, LSAT Technical Report 97-01, August 1999: 11). Also see Susan Sturm and Lani Guinier, "Affirmative Action: Reclaiming the Innovative Ideal," 84 *California Law Review* 953 (1966), footnotes 68, 69, 76–82.
76. Peter Sacks, "How Admissions Tests Hinder Access to Graduate and Professional Schools," *Chronicle of Higher Education* (June 8, 2001).
77. Law School Admissions Council, *What Is a Score Band?*
78. George B. Shepherd, "Lawyers Allowed: The Inefficient Racism of the ABA's Accreditation of Law Schools," *Journal of Legal Education* 53 (2003): 103–56.
79. "LSAT: A Testing 'Poll Tax' on Minority Law School Applicants," *FairTest Examiner* (Summer 2000).
80. Educational Testing Service, "GRE Guide to the Use of Scores, 1998–1999" (Princeton, N.J.: ETS, 1998).
81. Sacks, "How Admissions Tests Hinder Access."
82. R. R. Scott and M. E. Shaw, "Black and White Performance in Graduate School and Policy Implications for Using GRE Scores in Admission," *Journal of Negro Education* 54, 1 (1985): 14–23.
83. Ibid.
84. Richard O. Lempert, David L. Chambers, and Terry K. Adams, "The River Runs Through Law School," *Journal of Law and Social Inquiry* 25 (2000): 468.

85. Sacks, "How Admissions Tests Hinder Access."
86. R. Davidson and E. Lewis. "Affirmative Action and Other Special Consideration Admissions at the University of California, Davis, School of Medicine," *Journal of the American Medical Association* 278 (1997): 22–25.
87. Pinkney, *The Myth of Black Progress*, 155.
88. "Cadet Quotas" (1998). Available online at www.savannahmorning-news.com:80/smn/stories/060798/OPEDone.html.
89. Thomas Sowell, *Inside American Education: The Decline, the Deception, the Dogmas* (New York: Free Press, 1993).
90. Brown et al., *Whitewashing Race*, 117.
91. Theodore Cross, "The Myth That Preferential College Admissions Create High Black Student Dropout Rates," *Journal of Blacks in Higher Education* 1 (Autumn 1993): 73.
92. Brown et al., *Whitewashing Race*, 282, fn 51.
93. Bowen and Bok, *The Shape of the River*, 259.
94. Brown et al., *Whitewashing Race*, 116.
95. Thomas Kane, "Racial and Ethnic Preferences in College Admissions," in *The Black-White Test Score Gap*, ed. Christopher Jencks and Meredith Phillips (Washington, D.C.: Brookings Institution Press, 1998), 444–45.
96. Claude Steele, "Race and the Schooling of Black Americans," *Atlantic Monthly* 69 (April 1992): 68–78.
97. Massey et al., *The Source of the River*, 2.
98. Ibid., 16.
99. Steele, "Race and the Schooling."
100. Massey et al., *The Source of the River*, 42.
101. Ibid.
102. Conley, *Being Black*, 59.
103. Massey et al., *The Source of the River*, 43.
104. Ibid., 156.
105. Carnevale and Rose, *Socioeconomic Status, Race/Ethnicity*, 14.
106. Conley, *Being Black*, 72.
107. Jacqueline Fleming, *Blacks in College* (San Francisco: Jossey-Bass, 1984).
108. Brown et al., *Whitewashing Race*, 116.
109. Kunjufu, *Black Students, Middle Class Teachers*, 38.
110. John F. Dovidio, "Racial, Ethnic and Cultural Differences in Responding to Distinctiveness and Discrimination on Campus: Stigma and Common Group Identity," *Journal of Social Issues* (Spring 2001).

111. Brown et al., *Whitewashing Race*, 244.
112. Carnevale and Rose, *Socioeconomic Status, Race/Ethnicity*, 69, table 2.1.
113. Ibid.
114. Ibid.
115. Ibid.
116. Brown et al., *Whitewashing Race*, 282, fn 54.
117. Joe Feagin, Hernan Vera, and Nikitah Imani, *The Agony of Education: Black Students in White Colleges and Universities* (New York: Routledge, 1996).
118. Linda Wightman, "The Threat to Diversity in Legal Education: An Empirical Investigation," *New York University Law Review.* 72, 1 (1997): 1–53. Despite entering law schools with average LSATs considerably lower than whites and grades from college that are one standard deviation lower as well, black students graduate at rates that are not statistically significantly lower than whites: eighty percent as compared to ninety percent. Indeed, even among those blacks who wouldn't have been admitted under pure LSAT/UGPA criteria, seventy-eight percent (and eighty percent of all "preferenced" URMs) go on to graduate from the law schools they attend, hardly different from the eighty percent rate at which those who would have gotten in anyway graduate. This means that these students are not less capable than their more "qualified" counterparts, and also that something other than ability must explain lower black graduation rates relative to those of whites, since even those blacks who would have gotten in on pure merit graduate at a rate that is ten percentage points below whites, and are therefore *twice as likely* to fail to graduate as whites. What these data also indicate is that the LSAT and UGPA cannot accurately select better qualified black applicants as opposed to less qualified black applicants. This means that the marginal benefit of using only LSATs and grades from college in terms of getting a better quality pool of students of color, thereby preventing stigma, or merely boosting selectivity and net merit, or for whatever reason, is nil. Interestingly, there is also no statistically significant difference in bar passage rates between students who would have been rejected under a pure LSAT/college GPA analysis, but who were admitted thanks to affirmative action, and those whose scores would have won them admission from the outset.
119. George B. Shepherd, "Lawyers Allowed: The Inefficient Racism of the ABA's Accreditation of Law Schools," *Journal of Legal Education* 53 (2003): 103–56.

120. Ibid. Along these same lines, not only are black law school graduates equally capable upon completion of their legal education, but in fact, all the available evidence suggests they were equally qualified from the outset, even at the point of admission. Critics of affirmative action compare the entering credentials (as expressed in test scores and undergraduate grades) of white and black students in order to demonstrate the unfairness of affirmative action—the operative assumption being that if there is a large gap, there was substantial preference given to the students of color, and that therefore whites with far better "qualifications" were likely bumped to make way for them. But this position is untenable and incorrect for a couple of obvious reasons. To begin with, the credentials of those whites *not* admitted to a given school cannot be assumed equal to those whites who *were* admitted. In fact, if we assume that the students of color with marginal on-paper credentials (but who were admitted because of affirmative action) likely bumped out whites at the bottom of the white applicant pool in terms of merit, then we would have to assume that those whites were much more like the students of color who bumped them out than the whites who were admitted with top qualifications. In other words, the question is not how qualified were blacks relative to whites admitted, but whites *rejected*. Linda Wightman, formerly a research director with the Law School Admission Council, examined this issue, by comparing the entering credentials of whites whose grades placed them in the bottom tenth of their first-year classes in law school with the entering credentials of blacks in the lowest tenth of the class. She reasoned that these black students would have been the ones who most likely "needed" affirmative action to get in, and that these whites would have been very close, in terms of qualifications, to those whites edged out due to affirmative action. What she found was a very small gap in entering credentials—too small, in fact, to suggest a statistically significant difference in actual ability. On average, blacks in this group had an LSAT score of thirty-three (on the old forty-eight point scale), compared to thirty-six for whites, and a 3.03 undergraduate GPA, compared to 3.19 for whites (Linda Wightman, "Are Other Things Essentially Equal? An Empirical Investigation of the Consequences of Including Race as a Factor in Law School Admissions," 28 *Southwestern University Law Review* 1998: 19). Among whites predicted to finish in the bottom tenth of their first-year classes (based on LSAT and undergrad GPA), who would likely be the students "bumped"

because of affirmative action at top schools, there was no significant difference between them and the blacks predicted to be in the bottom tenth (who would likely represent the students who did the "bumping"). For African Americans in this group, the average LSAT was a 31.2, compared to 32.6 for whites—within the standard margin of error, indicating essentially no difference in predicted ability. Average GPAs for students in these groups were identical: 2.9 for both whites and blacks (Wightman, 1998: 26). Likewise, there was no significant difference in graduation rates for whites and blacks predicted to be in the bottom tenth of the class, ninety-one percent rates for blacks and ninety-six percent for whites (Wightman, 1998: 29).

121. Conley, *Being Black*, 73.
122. Bowen and Bok, *The Shape of the River*, 74–75.
123. Wightman, "Standardized Testing and Equal Access," 92.
124. Steinhorn and Diggs-Brown, *By the Color of Our Skin*, 47.
125. Rebecca Gordon, Della Piana Libero, and Terry Kelleher, *Facing the Consequences: An Examination of Racial Discrimination in U.S. Public Schools* (Oakland, Calif.: Applied Research Center, 2000), 17.
126. Oakes, *Keeping Track*, 98–101.
127. Orfield and Eaton, *Dismantling Desegregation*.
128. William Trent et al., "Justice, Equality of Educational Opportunity, and Affirmative Action in Higher Education," in *Compelling Interest: Examining the Evidence on Racial Dynamics in Colleges and Universities*, ed. Mitchell J. Chang et al. (Palo Alto: Stanford University Press, 2003), 37.
129. Conrad, "Affirmative Action and Admission."
130. Steele, "Race and the Schooling."
131. Katheryn K. Russell, *The Color of Crime: Racial Hoaxes, White Fear, Black Protectionism, Police Harassment and Other Macroaggressions* (New York: New York University Press, 1998), 7.
132. Expert Report of Claude M. Steele, in *Gratz v. Bollinger et al.*, 97-75321 E.D. Mich. (2001), 5–6. Available online at www.umich.edu/~urel/admissions/legal/expert.steele.html. Interestingly, stereotype threat does not only affect blacks. Steele and his colleagues have done similar experiments with other stereotyped groups and found similar results: for example, stereotype threat depresses female scores on math tests, due to negative beliefs that are quite common about girls and women and math; likewise, white males are negatively affected by stereotype threat when put in a competitive math

test situations against Asians, due to the belief that Asians do better on math.

133. Expert Report of David M. White, 18.
134. Claude Steele, "A Threat in the Air: How Stereotypes Shape Intellectual Identity and Performance," in *Confronting Racism: The Problem and the Response*, ed. Jennifer L. Eberhardt and Susan T. Fiske (London: Sage, 1998), 219.
135. Levin, "Social Psychological Evidence," 106.
136. Steele, "Race and the Schooling."
137. Massey et al., *The Source of the River*, 186–87.
138. Ibid., 196. These factors include high levels of concern over teacher perceptions, low confidence in the general ability of blacks academically, a tendency to identify not with their racial group but rather with "America" generally, and personal doubts about their own academic ability.
139. Levin, "Social Psychological Evidence," 107.
140. Steele, "Race and the Schooling."
141. Levin, "Social Psychological Evidence," 115.
142. Rinku Sen, *The Persistence of White Privilege and Institutional Racism in US Policy: A Report on US Government Compliance with the International Convention on the Elimination of All Forms of Racial Discrimination* (Oakland, Calif.: Transnational Racial Justice Initiative–Applied Research Center, 2001), 50.
143. Trial Testimony of Jay Rosner, in *Grutter v. Bollinger et al.* 97-75928 E.D. Mich. (February 6, 2001), 105.
144. Expert Report of David M. White, 13.
145. Trial Testimony of Jay Rosner, 125.
146. Sturm and Guinier, "Affirmative Action."
147. D. Lederman, "The Special Preferences Are Not Limited to Blacks," *Chronicle of Higher Education* (April 28, 1995): A-16–18.
148. Sturm and Guinier, "Affirmative Action."
149. "UCLA Chief Admits Possible Favoritism: Chancellor Charles Young Acknowledges Applicants Sponsored by Regents and Other Officials May Have Been Given Admissions Preferences," *Los Angeles Times*, March 17, 1996.
150. Kenneth R. Weiss, "UC Regents Decry but Keep Entrance Favors," *Los Angeles Times*, July 17, 1998.
151. James Fallows, "The Early Decision Racket," *Atlantic Monthly* (September 2001).

152. Shelby Steele, *The Content of Our Character: A New Vision of Race in America* (New York: St. Martin's Press, 1990); John McWhorter, *Losing the Race: Self-Sabotage in Black America* (New York: Free Press, 2000).

153. William Galston, "An Affirmative Action Status Report: Evidence and Options," *Philosophy and Public Policy* 17 (Winter/Spring 1997).

154. Grant Jerding, "Changes in Race Relations in the USA," *USA Today*, June 11, 1997.

155. Richard J. Herrnstein and Charles Murray, *The Bell Curve: Intelligence and Class Structure in American Life* (New York: Free Press, 1994).

156. Rowan, *Coming Race War in America*, 156.

157. Kinder and Sanders, *Divided by Color*, 127.

158. Fischer et al., *Inequality by Design*, 13.

159. Lee Cokorinos, *The Assault on Diversity: An Organized Challenge to Racial and Gender Justice* (Lanham, Md.: Rowman & Littlefield, 2003), 32.

160. Ibid., 36, 56.

161. *Chronicle of Higher Education* (July 28, 1995).

162. Harry J. Holzer and David Neumark, "Assessing Affirmative Action," *Journal of Economic Literature* 38 (2000); Michael Weinstein, "A Reassuring Scorecard for Affirmative Action," *New York Times*, October 17, 2000.

163. D'Souza, *The End of Racism*; Thernstrom and Thernstrom, *America in Black and White*.

164. Gary Mar, "Are Asians Model Minorities?" (2001). Available online at http://academic.udayton.edu/race/01race/model01.htm.

165. Stephen Steinberg, *The Ethnic Myth* (Boston: Beacon Press, 1989).

166. Fox Butterfield, "Why Asians Are Going to the Head of the Class," *New York Times* (education supplement), August 3, 1986.

167. U.S. Federal Glass Ceiling Commission, *Good for Business: Making Full Use of the Nation's Human Capital* (Washington, D.C.: Bureau of National Affairs, March 1995), 107.

168. U.S. Bureau of the Census, *Current Population Surveys* (Washington, D.C.: U.S. Government Printing Office, March 1997).

169. Vijay Prashad, *The Karma of Brown Folk* (Minneapolis: University of Minnesota Press, 2000), 75.

170. Fischer et al., *Inequality by Design*, 193.

171. Thernstrom and Thernstrom, *America in Black and White*, 535–36.

172. U.S. Bureau of the Census, *Household Income Data 1996, Current Population Surveys* (Washington, D.C.: U.S. Government Printing Office, 1996); U.S. Bureau of the Census, *Current Population Surveys* (Washington, D.C.: U.S. Government Printing Office, March 1997).

173. Terrance Reeves and Claudette Bennett, *The Asian and Pacific Islander Population in the United States: March 2002* (Washington, D.C.: U.S. Bureau of the Census, Current Population Reports, P-20-540, May 2003), 3.

174. Asian and Pacific Islander Center for Census Information and Services, *Our Ten Years of Growth: A Demographic Analysis of Asian and Pacific Islander Americans* (San Francisco: ACCIS, 1992).

175. U.S. Bureau of the Census, *Statistical Abstracts of the United States, 2002,* 122nd ed. (Washington, D.C.: U.S. Government Printing Office, 2002), 433, tables 652, 653.

176. Reeves and Bennett, *Asian and Pacific Islander Population,* 4.

177. Ibid., 2.

178. U.S. Bureau of Economic Analysis, *Survey of Current Business* (Washington, D.C.: U.S. Government Printing Office, May 1998).

179. U.S. Bureau of the Census, *Statistical Abstracts of the United States, 1998,* 118th ed. (Washington, D.C.: U.S. Government Printing Office, 1998), 31.

180. U.S. Bureau of the Census, *Statistical Abstracts 2002,* 41, table 36.

181. Chan Sucheng, *Asian Americans: An Interpretive History* (Boston: Twayne, 1991), 168.

182. U.S. Bureau of Labor Statistics, *News* "Average Annual Pay Levels in Metropolitan Areas," USDL 97-379 (Washington, D.C.: U.S. Department of Labor, October 30, 1997).

183. Reeves and Bennett, *Asian and Pacific Islander Population,* 7.

184. Annie E. Casey Foundation, *Kids Count Data on Asian, Native American and Hispanic Children: Findings from the 1990 Census* (Washington, D.C.: Annie E. Casey Foundation, 1994).

185. Nancy Rivera Brooks, "Study Attacks Belief in Asian American Affluence, Privilege," *San Jose Mercury News,* May 19, 1994.

186. Ann Scott Tyson, "Asian Americans Spurn Image as Model Minority," *Christian Science Monitor,* August 26, 1994.

187. Lieutenant James G. Foggo III, "Review of Data on Asian Americans" (Cape Canaveral, FL: Defense Equal Opportunity Management Institute, May 1993).

188. S. Hune and K. S. Chan, "Special Focus: Asian Pacific American Demographic and Educational Trends," in *Minorities in Higher Education,* ed. D. Carter and R. Wilson (Washington, D.C.: American Council on Education, 1997): 39–107.

189. "Asian Pacific Islanders Trail Whites in Earnings—Comparable Education Fails to Close the Gap," *Washington Post,* September 18, 1992.

190. Don Lee, "Asian Americans Finding Cracks in the Glass Ceiling," *Los Angeles Times*, July 15, 1998.
191. George Curry, "Resurrecting the NAACP," *Emerge* (March 1996).
192. McWhorter, *Losing the Race*; D'Souza, *The End of Racism*.
193. D'Souza, *The End of Racism*.
194. Henry Louis Gates, Jr., "Breaking the Silence," *New York Times*, August 1, 2004.
195. Waller, *Face to Face*, 89.
196. U.S. Department of Education, *Digest of Education Statistics*, 155, table 137.
197. Dinesh D'Souza, for example, made this argument in a debate with the author at Bowling Green State University, in Bowling Green, Ohio, in 1998.
198. Christopher Jencks and Meredith Phillips, letter response, *American Prospect* 42 (January–February 1999).
199. Valerie E. Lee and David T. Burkham, *Inequality at the Starting Gate: Social Background Differences in Achievement as Children Begin School* (Washington, D.C.: Economic Policy Institute, 2002).
200. U.S. Bureau of the Census, *Statistical Abstracts 1998*, 69, table 85.
201. Blau, *Race in the Schools*, 28–29.
202. Conley, *Being Black*, 10.
203. Ibid., 68, 72.
204. Feagin et al., *The Agony of Education*, xi–xii.
205. Carol Goodenow and Kathleen E. Grady, "The Relationship of School Belonging and Friends' Values to Academic Motivation Among Urban Adolescent Students," *Journal of Experimental Education* 62 (1993): 60–71; Brenda Major and Toni Schmader, "Coping with Stigma Through Psychological Disengagement," in *Prejudice: The Target's Perspective*, ed. Janet K. Swim and Charles Stangor (New York: Academic Press, 1998), 219–41; Kristin E. Voelkl, "Identification With School," *American Journal of Education* 105 (1997): 294–318. Despite claims by many on the right that blacks—especially youth—have less commitment to education, hard work, and other "mainstream values," the available evidence seems to contradict this notion. One mid-1990s questionnaire of black high school seniors found that black seniors were just as likely as white seniors to say that a good marriage and family life were "extremely important" life goals; thirty-two percent more likely than whites to say that professional success and accomplishment were "extremely important" life goals; twenty-six percent more likely than whites to say

"making a contribution to society" was extremely important; and seventy-five percent more likely than whites to say "being a leader in their community" was an extremely important life goal. These black seniors were also twenty-one percent more likely than whites to attend weekly religious services and almost twice as likely as whites to say that religion played a "very important role in their lives"; J. G. Bachman et al., *Monitoring the Future: Questionnaire Responses from the Nation's High School Seniors* (Ann Arbor, Mich.: Institute for Social Research, 1994).

206. Daniel Solorzano, "Mobility Aspirations Among Racial Minorities, Controlling for SES," *Sociology and Social Research* 75, 4 (1991): 182–88.

207. Philip J. Cook and Jens Ludwig, "Weighing the Burden of 'Acting White': Are There Race Differences in Attitudes Towards Education?" *Journal of Policy Analysis and Management* 16, 2 (Spring 1997): 256–78.

208. Massey et al., *The Source of the River*, 9.

209. Sarah Carr, "Coalition Says Study Rebuts Education Myths: Responses Demonstrate Commitment of Minority Students, Educators Say," *Milwaukee Journal Sentinel Online*, November 19, 2002. Available online at www.jsonline.com/news/metro/nov02/97244.

210. Catherine Gewertz, "No Racial Gap Seen in Students' School Outlook," *Education Week* (November 20, 2002).

211. U.S. Department of Education, *Digest of Education Statistics*, 139, table 118.

212. U.S. Department of Education, *The Condition of Education 2002*, 143, table 11-2 and calculations by the author.

213. Blau, *Race in the Schools*, 57–59.

214. U.S. Department of Education, *Digest of Education Statistics*, 30, table 25.

215. Blau, *Race in the Schools*, 84–85, 92–93.

216. U.S. Department of Education, *Digest of Education Statistics*, 30, table 25.

217. Cook and Ludwig, "Weighing the Burden."

218. U.S. Department of Education, *Digest of Education Statistics*, 31, table 26.

219. Ibid., 162, table 144.

220. Hartnett, "Income Gaps Persist Among Races"

221. Massey et al., *The Source of the River*, 52–61.

222. Ibid., 110.

223. U.S. Department of Education, *Digest of Education Statistics*, 169, table 152.
224. Cook and Ludwig, "Weighing the Burden."
225. Llagas, *Status and Trends*, 144, suppl. table 3.3a.
226. U.S. Department of Education, *The Condition of Education 2002*, 163, table 18-2.

NOTES TO CHAPTER FOUR

1. Tim Wise, "Is Sisterhood Conditional? White Women and the Roll-back of Affirmative Action," *National Women's Studies Association Journal* 10, 3 (Fall 1998): 1–26.
2. Mitchell J. Chang et al., *Compelling Interest: Examining the Evidence on Racial Dynamics in Colleges and Universities* (Palo Alto, Calif.: Stanford University Press, 2003), 197.
3. For an excellent demonstration of the benefits of campus diversity, however secondary I may consider such concerns to be, see "The Compelling Need for Diversity in Higher Education," Expert Report of Patricia Gurin, *Gratz et al. v. Bollinger et al.*, 97-75321 E.D. Mich., *Grutter et al. v. Bollinger et al.*, 97-75928 E.D. Mich., 2001. Although several conservative organizations criticized Gurin's report (though notably not in court), her rebuttals to their critiques are entirely persuasive. For those interested, the Gurin report and her rebuttals to her critics, as well as other reports relevant to the Michigan cases, can be found at a special subsite of the university's main Web site: http://www. umich.edu/~urel/admissions.
4. As just one example, consider the study by the Harvard Civil Rights Project, which asked these kinds of questions of law students. Gary Orfield and Dean Whitla, "Diversity and Legal Education: Student Experiences in Leading Law Schools" (Cambridge, Mass.: Harvard Civil Rights Project, August 1999). For that matter, one may also consult the Gurin study (above) developed for the University of Michigan's defense of its affirmative action policies before the Supreme Court.
5. Pincus, *Reverse Discrimination*, 5–6; Wise, "Is Sisterhood Conditional?" 10.
6. Geoffrey Garin and Guy Molyneaux, "Defending Affirmative Action: Communicating a Winning Message" (Washington, D.C.: Peter D. Hart Research Associates, internal report, 1996); Wise, "Is Sisterhood Conditional?"

7. Walter Stephan, *Reducing Prejudice and Stereotyping in Schools* (New York: Teachers College Press, 1999).
8. Sylvia Hurtado et al., "Enhancing Campus Climates for Racial/Ethnic Diversity Through Educational Policy and Practice," *Review of Higher Education* 21, 3 (1998): 279–302.
9. Orfield and Whitla, "Diversity and Legal Education."
10. Bowen and Bok, *The Shape of the River.*
11. Dinesh D'Souza has made this point, in one form or another, in several debates with this author, dating back to 1995.
12. Carlos E. Cortes, "Beyond Affirmative Action," *MultiCultural Review* 5, 1 (March 1996).

INDEX